Easy 1-2-3® for Windows™

Shelley O'Hara

Publisher: David P. Ewing

Associate Publisher: Rick Ranucci

Operations Manager: Sheila Cunningham

Publishing Plan Manager: Thomas H. Bennett

Book Design: Amy Peppler-Adams

Production Team: Claudia Bell, Danielle Bird, Julie Brown, Jodie Cantwell, Tim Cox, Bob LaRoche, Jay Lesandrini, Linda Koopman, Wendy Ott, Sandra Shay, Marcella Thompson, Donna Winter

Production Editor
Cindy Morrow

Technical Editor
Lynda Fox

Novice Reviewer
Stacey Beheler

All terms mentioned in this book that are known to be trademarks or service marks have been appropriately capitalized. Que cannot attest to the accuracy of this information. Use of a term in this book should not be regarded as affecting the validity of any trademark or service mark.

Lotus and 1-2-3 are registered trademarks of Lotus Development Corporation.

Microsoft Windows is a trademark of Microsoft Corporation.

Shelley O'Hara is a Title Manager at Que Corporation. She is the author of 17 books in the *Easy* series, including the best-selling *Easy WordPerfect*, *Easy Windows*, and *Easy 1-2-3*. She is also the coauthor of *Real Men Use DOS*. Ms. O'Hara received her bachelor's degree from the University of South Carolina and her master's degree from the University of Maryland.

Contents

Easy 1-2-3 for Windows

Contents

ix

The Basics

Easy 1-2-3 for Windows

Dear Reader:

If you are a beginning user and intimidated by computers, this book is written for you. This book is set up to make it as easy as possible to learn how to use a program such as 1-2-3 for Windows.

First, this book explains all terms and concepts so that they are easy to understand. You aren't expected to know all the buzzwords of computing.

Second, this book doesn't cover every single 1-2-3 for Windows feature. It starts with the basics and then moves on to cover the features you'll use most often in your day-to-day work.

Third, this book includes easy-to-follow steps for each procedure. It's simple to follow along with the sample exercise or to use the steps as a review.

Fourth, you don't need to worry that you might do something wrong and ruin a document or the computer. This book points out mistakes that you might make and shows you how to avoid them. This book explains how to escape from a situation when you change your mind during a procedure.

I hope that you learn a lot from this book—enough to get started and build your confidence. Armed with that confidence, you'll be ready to create any type of worksheet.

Sincerely,

Shelley O'Hara

What Is 1-2-3 for Windows?

1-2-3 for Windows is a *spreadsheet program*—an electronic accountant's pad. Rather than total figures using a pencil and column-ruled paper, you enter data into a 1-2-3 for Windows worksheet. Then you can manipulate the data in that worksheet. With a spreadsheet program, you can perform simple mathematical operations—addition, subtraction, multiplication, and division—as well as calculate complex equations.

Using 1-2-3 for Windows, you can keep track of facts (for instance, client information) and figures (for instance, sales results). You can create simple worksheets or complex financial models. Here are some of the worksheets you can create with 1-2-3 for Windows:

- Home Budget
- Business Budget
- Sales Report
- Business Expense Report
- Financial Report
- Check Register
- Inventory List
- Personnel List
- Client List
- Grade List

Sure, you can create all of these worksheets without using a spreadsheet program. But creating them is a lot faster and easier when you use 1-2-3 for Windows. For example, you can use 1-2-3 for Windows to

Calculate. One advantage of doing your worksheets in 1-2-3 for Windows is how easily you can write simple formulas to add, subtract, multiply, and divide. You tell 1-2-3 for Windows what numbers to use, and you can depend on the program to calculate the results correctly every time.

Change data and recalculate. You can change, add, or delete data, and 1-2-3 for Windows recalculates results automatically. If you change the sales figures for July, 1-2-3 automatically recalculates the total for the year. There's no erasing and rewriting when you forget a crucial figure. And you don't have to manually refigure all the amounts when you do make changes or additions.

Rearrange data. With your worksheet on-screen, you can add or delete a column or row. You can copy and move data from one spot to another.

Repeat information. You can copy text, a value, or a formula to another place in the worksheet. Suppose, for example, that in your monthly budget worksheet, you total the expenses for each month. You could write a formula that calculated January's totals, and then copy this formula for February through December.

Reverse changes. Using the Edit Undo command, you can restore data that you just deleted, moved, or copied.

Change the format of data. You can format your results in many ways. You can tell 1-2-3 to display a number with dollar signs, as a percent, or as a date. You can tell the program to align text left, right, or center.

Add enhancements. The heart of 1-2-3 for Windows is its number-crunching capabilities. But the *results* are what you use. You can make those results stand out—by adding a drop shadow, underlining data, adding a background shade, and numerous other methods.

How to Use This Book

This book is set up so that you can use it several different ways:

- You can read the book from start to finish. Or you can start reading at any point in the book.

- You can experiment with one exercise, many exercises, or all exercises.

- You can look up specific tasks you want to accomplish, such as copying a cell.

- You can flip through the book, looking at the Before and After pictures, to find specific tasks.

- You can read just the exercise, just the review, or both the exercise and review parts.

- You can read any part of the exercises you want. You can read all the text—both the steps to follow and the explanation of the steps. You can read only the text in red to learn just the keystrokes to press. You can read just the explanation to understand what happens during a particular step.

- You can refer to the alphabetical listing of tasks at the beginning of the Task/Review part to locate specific tasks easily.

Task section

The Task section includes numbered steps that detail how to accomplish certain tasks—such as saving a worksheet. The numbered steps walk you through a specific example so that you can learn the task by *doing* it. Blue text below the numbered steps explains the concept further.

Oops! notes

You may find that you performed a task, such as underlining text, that you do not want after all. The Oops! notes tell you how to undo each procedure. In addition, The Oops! notes also may explain how to get out of a situation, such as how to close a Help screen. By showing you how to reverse nearly every procedure or get out of nearly every mode, these notes allow you to use 1-2-3 for Windows more confidently.

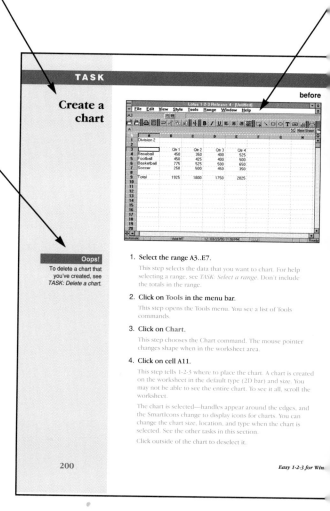

TASK

before

Create a chart

Oops!
To delete a chart that you've created, see *TASK: Delete a chart.*

1. **Select the range A3..E7.**

   This step selects the data that you want to chart. For help selecting a range, see *TASK: Select a range.* Don't include the totals in the range.

2. **Click on Tools in the menu bar.**

   This step opens the Tools menu. You see a list of Tools commands.

3. **Click on Chart.**

   This step chooses the Chart command. The mouse pointer changes shape when in the worksheet area.

4. **Click on cell A11.**

   This step tells 1-2-3 where to place the chart. A chart is created on the worksheet in the default type (2D bar) and size. You may not be able to see the entire chart. To see it all, scroll the worksheet.

   The chart is selected—handles appear around the edges, and the SmartIcons change to display icons for charts. You can change the chart size, location, and type when the chart is selected. See the other tasks in this section.

   Click outside of the chart to deselect it.

200

Easy 1-2-3 for Win

Before and After screens

Each task includes Before and After screens that show how the computer screen looks before and after you follow the numbered steps in the Task sections.

Review section

After you learn a procedure by following a specific example, you can refer to the Review section for a quick summary of the task. The Review section gives you generic steps for completing a task so that you can apply those steps to your own work. You can use these steps as a quick reference to refresh your memory about how to perform procedures.

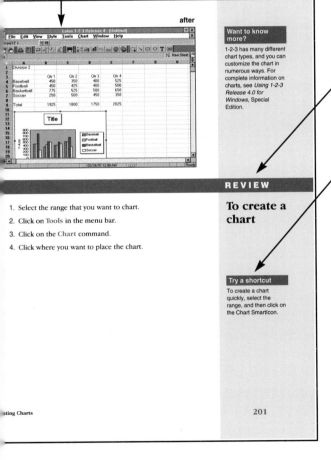

after

Want to know more?

1-2-3 has many different chart types, and you can customize the chart in numerous ways. For complete information on charts, see *Using 1-2-3 Release 4.0 for Windows*, Special Edition.

REVIEW

1. Select the range that you want to chart.
2. Click on Tools in the menu bar.
3. Click on the Chart command.
4. Click where you want to place the chart.

To create a chart

Try a shortcut

To create a chart quickly, select the range, and then click on the Chart SmartIcon.

Other notes

Many tasks also contain other short notes that tell you a little more about each procedure. These notes define terms, explain other options, refer you to other sections when applicable, and so on.

How to Follow an Exercise

1-2-3 for Windows is flexible because it allows you to perform a task in many different ways. For consistency, this book makes certain assumptions about how your computer is set up and how you use 1-2-3 for Windows. As you follow along with each exercise, keep the following key points in mind:

- This book assumes that you followed the default installation. This book assumes that you have installed a printer and that you have not changed any program defaults.

- This book assumes that you use the mouse to select commands and cells. Remember that you also can access commands using the keyboard. (To learn more about the keyboard, see the *Keyboard Guide* in the Reference part of this book.)

- In the Task/Review sections, this book assumes that you are starting from the Before screen. If this screen contains any data, begin by typing this text.

- Only the Before and After screens are illustrated. Screens are not shown for every step within an exercise. Where necessary, the steps explain message boxes and dialog boxes that appear on-screen.

- Each exercise is independent. That is, you don't have to complete any preceding exercises to follow along with the exercise you want.

- As the tasks get more complex, the examples are also more complex. In some examples, the columns have been widened and the cells formatted.

Important Stuff to Remember

Now that you know the key to the book, you have to keep only a few other things in mind. The information covered in the following sections pertain to the basics of using 1-2-3 for Windows—the do-it-all-the-time kind of things. Take a quick look through these sections before you get started with the program.

Using a Mouse

Using the mouse is the easiest and most natural way to learn 1-2-3 for Windows and other Windows programs. This book assumes that you are using a mouse. (If you really want to use the keyboard, however, you'll find some keyboard guidance in the *Keyboard Guide* in the Reference part of this book.)

There are four types of mouse actions:

Action Name	What You Do
Point	Move the on-screen mouse pointer to an item.
Click	Point to an item, press the left mouse button, and release the mouse button.
Double-click	Point to an item and press the left mouse button twice in rapid succession.
Drag	Point to an item. Press and hold down the left mouse button and then move the mouse. Once the item you are dragging is where you want it, release the mouse button.

Keep these terms in mind as you follow a task.

Understanding the 1-2-3 for Windows Screen

After you start the program, you see the program window and a blank worksheet window. If you want to start the program and follow along, see *TASK: Start 1-2-3 for Windows*, which is the first task in the Task/Review part.

Oops!

If you double-click the mouse and nothing happens, it may be that you did not click quickly enough. Try again.

The main window contains these elements:

- Title bar
- Menu bar
- Edit line
- SmartIcons
- Status bar
- Control menu icon

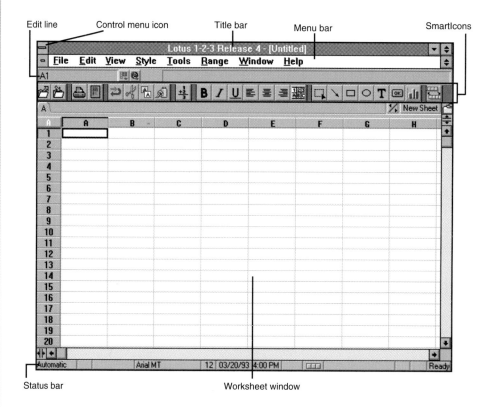

Edit line   Control menu icon   Title bar   Menu bar   SmartIcons

Status bar   Worksheet window

The program's *title bar* displays the name of the program. At the far left of this bar is the *Control menu icon*. You can double-click on this icon to exit the program.

The *menu bar* appears under the title bar. This line displays the menu names. To select a menu command, see *TASK: Choose a menu command*.

The *edit line* includes the selection indicator, the navigator button, and the contents box. The *selection indicator* tells you the address of the current selection. You can click on the *navigator button* to display a list of *named ranges*. (Naming ranges is covered in *TASK: Name a range* in the Task part of this book.) The *contents box* displays the contents of the selected cell.

The *SmartIcons* are shortcuts for common tasks.

The *status bar* displays the current numeric format, type-face, point size, and other items in separate panels. The status bar also displays the date and time, as well as status indicators such as Ready, Value, and Label.

The Worksheet Window

The main part of the 1-2-3 for Windows screen is the work area, which looks like this:

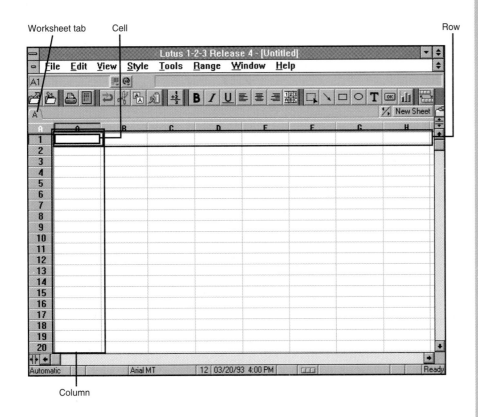

You can display worksheets within the work area.

A *worksheet* is a grid of columns and rows. A 1-2-3 for Windows worksheet has 256 columns and 8,192 rows.

Worksheets are identified with letters, which appear in the worksheet tab. The first worksheet is A. You store worksheets in a *file*. One file can include up to 256 worksheets.

Columns are identified with letters (A-Z, AA-AZ, BA-BZ, and so on through IV) across the worksheet.

Rows are numbered 1 through 8,192 down the worksheet.

A *cell* is the intersection of a column and row. You can select a cell—make it the *current cell*—by clicking on it with the mouse. You can also use the arrow keys to select a cell. (Selecting a cell is explained in the next section.)

A cell is identified by an address. An address includes these elements:

- The worksheet letter
- The column letter
- The row number

A:A1 is an example of a cell address. This cell address tells you that you are working with the first worksheet (A:), column A, and row 1. If you have only one worksheet as part of the file, you won't see A: as part of the address.

Selecting a Cell

To use the mouse to select a cell, click on that cell.

You also can use arrow keys to select the current cell on-screen. Here is a list of the most common keys and key combinations:

To move	Press
One cell right	→
One screen right	Tab
One cell left	←
One screen left	Shift-Tab
One row up	↑
One row down	↓
To column A	Home
To the first cell in worksheet	Ctrl-Home

Saving and Retrieving Your Work

All of your work is stored *temporarily* in memory. It's as if you have a shopping list in your head. Until you commit the list to paper, you may forget some or all of the items. The same is true with 1-2-3 for Windows. Until you save the worksheet in a file, you can lose all or part of your work.

Saving the worksheet doesn't commit it to paper like the shopping list. Saving the worksheet puts a copy of the worksheet on a disk. The worksheet is stored in a file, and the file has a distinct name. Then when you need the worksheet again, you can retrieve the file from the disk.

1-2-3 for Windows does not automatically save your work; you need to save it—preferably every 5 or 10 minutes. If you don't save your work, you could lose it. Suppose that you have been working on a worksheet for a few hours. Then the electricity is turned off unexpectedly—an air conditioning repair person at your office shorts out the power or a thunderstorm hits. Any number of things can cause a power loss. If you haven't saved all your hard work, it's gone.

See the section *Managing Files* in the Task/Review part for information on saving and opening worksheet files.

Task/Review

Entering and Editing Data

Managing Files

Formatting

More Editing

More Formatting

Printing

Creating Charts

Easy 1-2-3 for Windows

Entering and Editing Data

This section includes the following tasks:

Start 1-2-3 for Windows

Choose a menu command

Exit 1-2-3 for Windows

Get help

Enter text

Enter a number

Enter a date

Enter a time

Add cells

Subtract cells

Multiply cells

Divide two cells

Overwrite a cell

Edit a cell

Erase a cell

Copy a cell

Move a cell

Go to a specific cell

Use undo

Select a range

Start 1-2-3 for Windows

before

C:\>

1. **Turn on the computer and monitor.**

   Every computer has a different location for its power switch. Check the side, the front, and the back of your computer. Your monitor might have a separate power switch; if so, flip on this switch, also.

2. **If necessary, respond to the prompts for date and time.**

   Some computers ask you to enter the current date and time. (Many of the newer models enter the time and date automatically. If you aren't prompted for these entries, don't worry.)

   If you are prompted, type the current date and press Enter. Then type the current time and press Enter.

3. **Type win and press Enter.**

   Win is the command to start Windows. You see Program Manager on-screen. Program Manager is an application that comes with Microsoft Windows.

4. **Double-click on the group icon for Lotus Applications**

   To double-click, move the mouse pointer to the Lotus Applications icon and click the left mouse button twice in rapid succession. This step opens the Lotus Applications program window.

Easy 1-2-3 for Windows

after

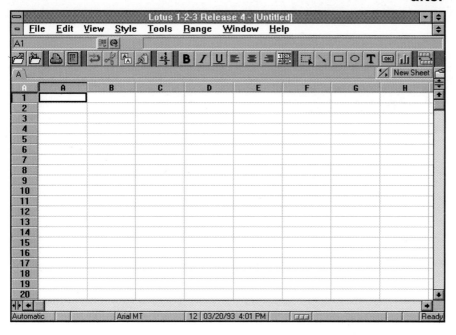

Exit 1-2-3 for Windows

To exit 1-2-3 for Windows, see *TASK: Exit 1-2-3 for Windows*.

5. Double-click on the program icon for **1-2-3 for Windows**.

   This step starts the 1-2-3 for Windows program. A blank worksheet appears on-screen.

REVIEW

1. Turn on your computer and monitor.

2. Respond to the prompts for the date and time, if necessary.

3. Type **win** and press **Enter**.

4. Double-click on the group icon for **Lotus Applications**.

5. Double-click on the program icon for **1-2-3 for Windows**.

To start 1-2-3 for Windows

Install the program

To start the program, it must first be installed. See your 1-2-3 manual or *Using 1-2-3 Release 4.0 for Windows*, Special Edition, to learn how to install the program.

before

Choose a menu command

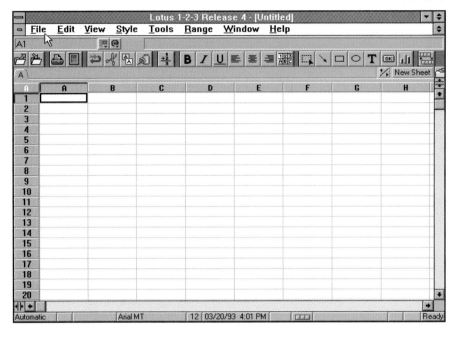

1. Point to **File** in the menu bar and click the left mouse button.

   This step opens the File menu. You see a list of File commands. The title bar displays a short description of the command that is highlighted on the menu.

2. Point to **Exit** and click the left mouse button.

   This step chooses and executes the command. You exit 1-2-3 for Windows.

after

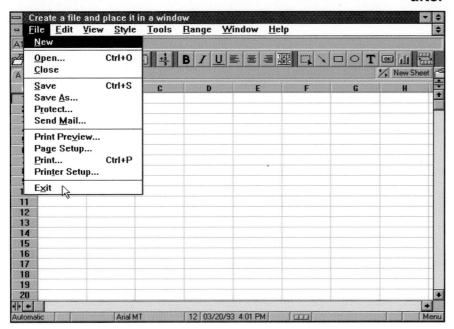

Shortcut keys and SmartIcons

You can access some commands by using shortcut keys, which are listed next to the command name, or by using SmartIcons. This book points out the shortcut and SmartIcons for each task.

REVIEW

1. Click on the menu name.

2. Click on the command name.

To choose a menu command

Dialog boxes?

When you choose some commands, you are asked for more information. In these cases, you see a *dialog box.* Here you type information (such as a file name) in text boxes, select options (check boxes or option buttons), or select items from a list. After you make the selections, click on OK to execute the command.

Entering and Editing Data

25

Exit 1-2-3 for Windows

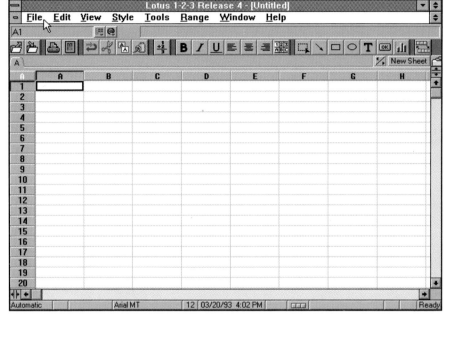

Oops!

To restart 1-2-3 for Windows, see *TASK: Start 1-2-3 for Windows*.

1. Point to **File** in the menu bar and click the left mouse button.

   This step opens the File menu. You see a list of File commands.

2. Point to **Exit** and click the left mouse button.

   This step chooses the Exit command. You return to the Windows Program Manager.

   Follow steps 3 through 5 if you want to exit Windows and return to DOS.

3. In the Program Manager, point to **File** and click the left mouse button.

   This step opens the File menu.

4. Point to **Exit Windows** and click the left mouse button.

   This step chooses the Exit Windows command. On-screen you see the Exit Windows dialog box.

5. Point to **OK** and click the left mouse button.

   This step confirms that you do want to exit. You are returned to DOS. You see the prompt C:\> on-screen.

after

```
C:\>
```

Save a worksheet

If you have typed any data or made any changes to the worksheet, you are prompted to save the changes before you exit. To learn more about saving files, look at the section "Managing Files."

REVIEW

To exit 1-2-3 for Windows

1. Click on **File** in the menu bar.

2. Click on the **Exit** command.

   To exit Windows, follow steps 3 through 5.

3. Click on **File** in the menu bar.

4. Click on the **Exit Windows** command.

5. Click on **OK**.

Get help

before

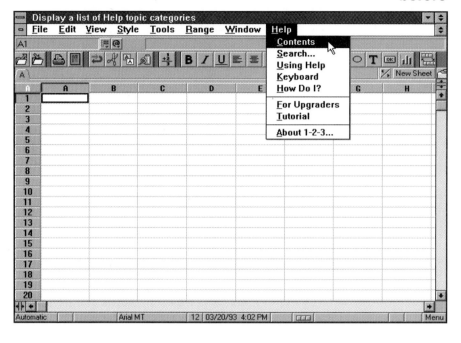

To quickly shut the Help window, double-click on the Control menu icon. The Control menu icon is the small bar to the left of the Help window's title bar.

1. Point to **Help** in the menu bar and click the left mouse button.

   This step opens the Help menu. On-screen you see a list of Help menu options.

2. Point to **Contents** and click the left mouse button.

   This step chooses the Contents command. You see the Help Contents list. When the mouse pointer is on a topic for which you can get help, the pointer changes to a hand with pointing finger.

3. Point to **Basics** and click the left mouse button.

   This step selects the category for which you want help. You see a list of topics.

4. Point to the topic **Entering Data** and click the left mouse button.

   This step chooses the topic and displays information about entering data. You may have to scroll the Help window to see all of the information, and the size and location of the Help window may vary from the one shown in the After screen.

   When you are finished, close the Help window.

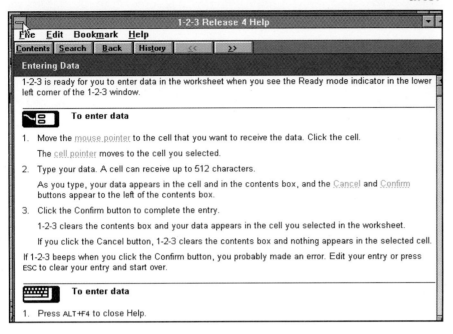

5. Point to **File** in the Help window and click the left mouse button.

   This step opens the File menu.

6. Point to **Exit** and click the left mouse button.

   This step chooses the Exit command and closes the Help window.

REVIEW

To get help

1. Click on **Help** in the menu bar.

2. Click on the **Contents** command.

3. Click on the category you want.

4. Click on the topic you want.

5. To close Help, click on **File** in the Help window menu bar.

6. Click on the **Exit** command.

Try a shortcut

Press the F1 key as a shortcut for steps 1 and 2.

Enter text

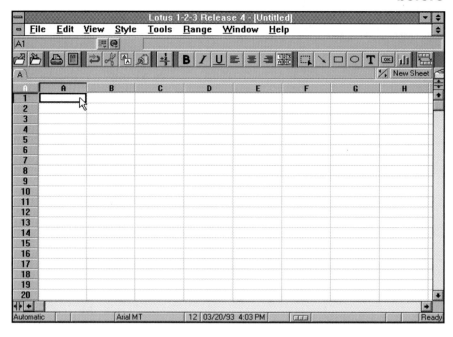

1. **Point to cell A1 and click the left mouse button.**

   This step makes A1 the current cell. The current cell on a worksheet appears with a bold border. You see `A1` in the selection indicator. In the status bar, you see `Ready`. This mode indicator means that 1-2-3 is ready to accept an entry.

   Each cell in a spreadsheet has a unique name. The cell name is formed by combining the worksheet letter (if the file contains more than one worksheet) and column and row locations into one description. For example, A:A1 describes the intersection of column A and row 1 in worksheet A.

2. **Type Sales.**

   This is the title of your worksheet. The mode indicator changes to `Label`, which indicates that you are entering a label (text).

3. **Press Enter.**

   Pressing Enter accepts the text and enters it into the cell. The cell pointer remains in cell A1. Note that in the contents box, the entry is preceded by an apostrophe. An apostrophe indicates that this entry is a label. 1-2-3 enters the apostrophe automatically.

   Note that the entry is left aligned. Left alignment is the default format for labels. To change this format, see the tasks on formatting the worksheet later in this book.

after

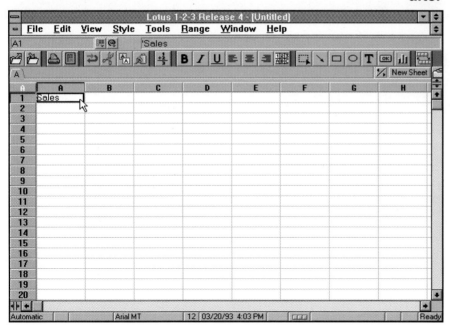

You also can use the arrow keys to select a cell. And you can press any of the arrow keys to accept the entry and move the cell pointer.

REVIEW

1. Click on the cell that you want to enter text into.

2. Type the text.

3. Press **Enter** or any arrow key.

To enter text

Make a mistake?

If you make a mistake when typing the entry, use the Backspace key to correct the entry. The entry is not placed in the cell until you press Enter or an arrow key.

Entering and Editing Data

Enter a number

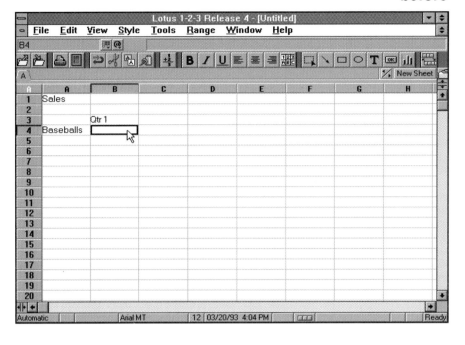

1. **Point to cell B4 and click the left mouse button.**

    This step makes B4 the current cell. You see B4 in the selection indicator; The mode indicator, Ready, tells you that 1-2-3 is ready to accept an entry.

2. **Type 10980.**

    The value, 10980, appears in the contents box and in the cell. The mode indicator changes to Value. If you make a mistake, use the Backspace key to correct the entry. The entry is not placed in the cell until you press Enter or an arrow key.

3. **Press ↓.**

    Pressing ↓ accepts the entry, enters the value into the cell, and moves the cell pointer to cell B5.

    Note that the entry is right aligned and that no decimal places, commas, or dollar signs are displayed—this is the default format for numbers. (You can change this format. See the tasks in the formatting section of this book.)

after

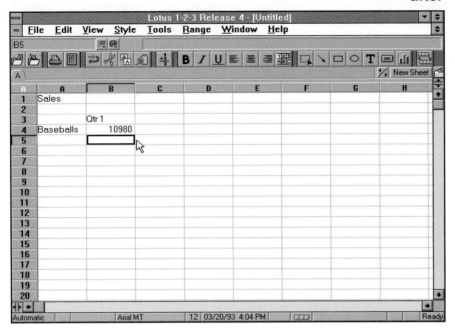

To enter a negative number, type a minus sign, and then type the number.

REVIEW

1. Click on the cell that you want to enter the number into.

2. Type the number.

3. Press **Enter** or any arrow key.

To enter a number

Enter a date

```
┌─────────────────────────────────────────────────────────────┐
│              Lotus 1-2-3 Release 4 - [Untitled]        ▼ ▲    │
│  File  Edit  View  Style  Tools  Range  Window  Help      ▲   │
│  A4                                                           │
│  [toolbar icons]  B / U ≡ ≡ ≡          \ □ ○ T [OK] [ill]    │
│  A                                              New Sheet     │
│      A        B       C     D      E     F     G     H        │
│  1  Business Expenses                                         │
│  2                                                            │
│  3  Date      Expense                                         │
│  4                                                            │
│  5                                                            │
│  6                                                            │
│  ...                                                          │
│  20                                                           │
│  Automatic        Arial MT    12  03/20/93  4:05 PM    Ready  │
└─────────────────────────────────────────────────────────────┘
```

Oops!

If you don't see a date on-screen, you may have typed the function incorrectly. Delete the entry and try again.

1. **Point to cell A4 and click the left mouse button.**

   This step makes A4 the current cell.

2. **Type @DATE(93,6,18).**

   1-2-3 treats dates in a particular way. If you just type the date without using a special entry method, 1-2-3 thinks that the date is a numerical value. For instance, if you type **6-18-93**, 1-2-3 interprets the entry as 6 *minus* 18 *minus* 93. 1-2-3 calculates this equation and displays the result (–101) in the cell. If you enter a date incorrectly, you see the results of a formula or ERR in the cell.

   You must use a special *function* to enter dates. @DATE is one function that you can use. Inside the parentheses, you enter the year, the month, and the date, all separated by commas.

   Note that there are no spaces between the function name and the parentheses, or between the numbers and the commas.

3. **Press Enter.**

   Pressing Enter confirms the entry. 1-2-3 translates the function and returns a number. Dates are stored as serial numbers. The numbering starts with 1 (January 1, 1900) and continues. 1-2-3 uses this format so that you can perform mathematical operations on dates—such as subtract two dates.

   Next you must format the cell so that it appears as a date.

Easy 1-2-3 for Windows

after

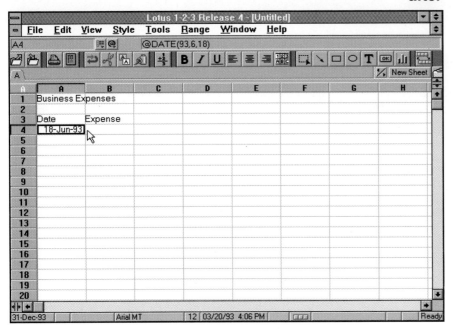

4. Click on the number format list in the status bar.

   The number format list is the first panel in the status bar and probably displays Automatic. You see a list of number formats.

5. Click on the format **31-Dec-93**.

   This step selects the format you want to use. In the cell you see 18-Jun-93. In the contents box, however, you see the date function.

1. Move the cell pointer to the cell in which you want to enter the date.

2. Type **@DATE(*yy*,*mm*,*dd*)**. Substitute the year for *yy*, the month for *mm*, and the day for *dd*.

3. Press **Enter**.

4. Click on the number format list in the status bar.

5. Click on the date format that you want to use.

See asterisks?

If asterisks (*) appear in the column, the entry is too large to fit in the column. You must change the column width so that the date can fit. See *TASK: Set column width.*

To enter a date

What is a panel?

The status bar includes several panels (areas) that let you change the format, the font, and several other things.

Enter a time

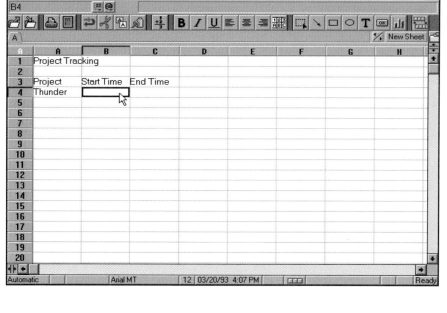

Oops!

If you don't see a time on-screen, you may have typed the function incorrectly. Delete the entry and try again.

1. **Point to cell B4 and click the left mouse button.**

   This step makes B4 the current cell.

2. **Type @TIME(8,0,0).**

   1-2-3 treats times in a particular way. If you just type the time without using a special entry method, 1-2-3 tries to enter the time as a *value*. You may see the result of a calculation or ERR in the cell.

   You must use a special function to enter times. @TIME is one of the functions you can use. Inside the parentheses, you enter the hour, the minutes, and the seconds, all separated by commas.

3. **Press Enter.**

   Pressing Enter confirms the entry. 1-2-3 translates the function and returns a number. Time is stored as a fraction of a 24-hour period, and 1-2-3 uses this format so that you can perform mathematical operations on times (subtract two times, for instance).

   Next you must format the cell so that it appears as a time.

after

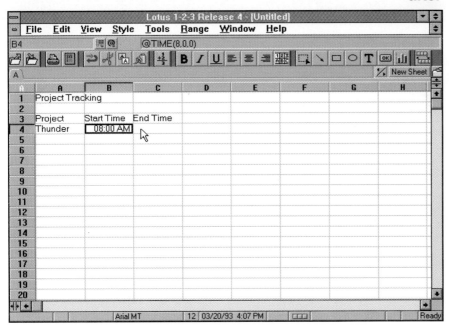

4. Click on the number format list in the status bar.

   The number format list is the first panel in the status bar and probably displays `Automatic`. You see a list of number formats.

5. Click on the format **11:59 AM**.

   This step selects the format you want to use. In the cell you see `08:00 AM`, but in the contents box, you see the time function.

REVIEW

1. Move the cell pointer to the cell you want to enter the time into.

2. Type **@TIME(*hh,mm,ss*)**. Substitute the hour for *hh*, the minutes for *mm*, and the seconds for *ss*. Use a 24-hour clock.

3. Press **Enter**.

4. Click on the number format list in the status bar.

5. Click on the time format you want to use.

To enter a time

Add cells

before

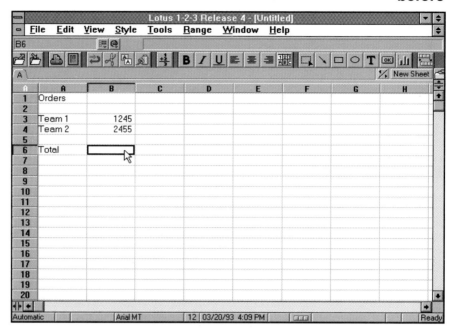

1. **Point to cell B6 and click the left mouse button.**

   This step makes B6 the current cell. The answer to the equation will appear in this cell.

2. **Press +.**

   This step tells 1-2-3 that you want to enter a formula. The mode indicator changes to Value.

   To add the contents of two or more cells, you create an addition formula. You point to the cells you want to include in this formula.

3. **Point to cell B3 and click the left mouse button.**

   This step selects cell B3, which is the first cell that you want to include in the addition formula. You see +B3 in the contents box and in the cell.

   You also can use the arrow keys instead of the mouse to point to the cell.

4. **Press +.**

   The + sign this time is the operator. It tells 1-2-3 which mathematical operation you want to perform—in this case, addition.

after

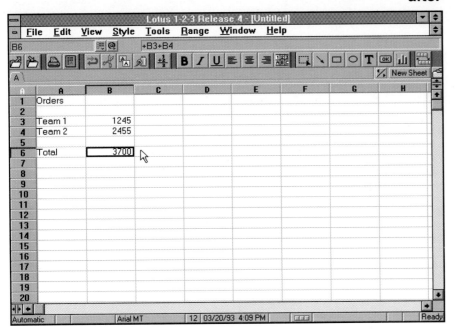

Why use a formula?

You could just type values into the formula, but then if you change the cell contents, the formula will be incorrect. Because the formula references the cells that contain values, the formula changes when you change the values in the cells.

5. Point to cell B4 and click the left mouse button.

This step selects B4, the second cell that you want to include. You see +B3+B4 in the contents box and in the cell.

6. Press **Enter**.

Pressing Enter tells 1-2-3 that you are finished with the addition formula. You see the result of the formula in cell B6. The contents box displays the formula—not the result.

Use @SUM

You can use the @SUM function to sum values, also. See *TASK: Total cells with the @SUM function.*

REVIEW

To add cells

1. Click on the cell in which you want to enter the formula.

2. Press +.

3. Select the first cell you want to include in the formula.

4. Press +.

5. Select the next cell you want to include in the formula.

6. Continue pressing the operator key (+) and selecting cells until you include all the cells you want.

7. Press **Enter**.

Entering and Editing Data

Subtract cells

before

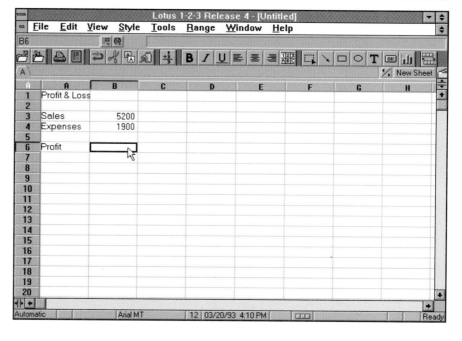

1. **Point to cell B6 and click the left mouse button.**

   This step makes B6 the current cell.

2. **Press +.**

   This step tells 1-2-3 that you want to enter a formula. The mode indicator changes to Value. You select the cells that you want to include in this formula.

3. **Point to cell B3 and click the left mouse button.**

   This step selects cell B3, which is the first cell that you want to include in the formula. You see +B3 in the contents box and in the cell.

   You also can use the arrow keys to point to the cell.

4. **Press –.**

   The – sign is the operator. It tells 1-2-3 which mathematical operation you want to perform—in this case, subtraction. You see +B3- in the contents box and in the cell.

5. **Point to cell B4 and click the left mouse button.**

   This step selects B4, the second cell that you want to include. You see +B3-B4 in the contents box and in the cell.

after

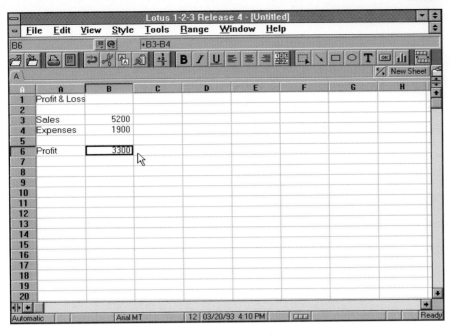

Why use a formula?

You could just type values into the formula, but then if you change the cell contents, the formula will be incorrect. Because the formula references the cells that contain values, the formula changes when you change the values in the cells.

6. Press **Enter**.

Pressing Enter tells 1-2-3 that you are finished with the formula. You see the result of the formula in the cell. The contents box displays the formula—not the result.

You can include any cells in your subtraction formula. They do not have to be next to each other.

To subtract cells

1. Click on the cell that you want to enter the subtraction formula into.

2. Press +.

3. Select the first cell you want to include.

4. Press –.

5. Select the second cell you want to include.

6. Continue typing the operator (–) and selecting cells until you include all the cells you want.

7. Press **Enter**.

Multiply cells

before

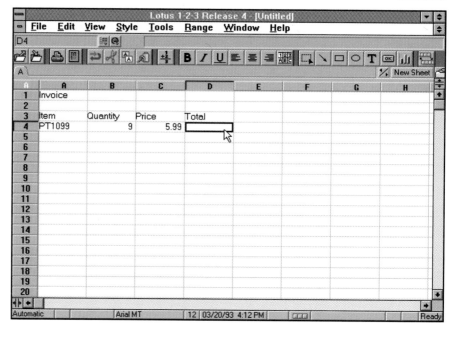

Oops!

To delete an entry, choose Edit Undo immediately after typing the entry.

1. **Point to cell D4 and click the left mouse button.**

   This step makes D4 the current cell. This cell is where you want to place the formula.

2. **Press +.**

   This step tells 1-2-3 that you want to enter a formula. The mode indicator changes to Value.

3. **Point to cell B4 and click the left mouse button.**

   This step selects cell B4, which is the first cell that you want to include in the formula. You see +B4 in the contents box and in the cell.

4. **Press *.**

   The * sign is the operator. It tells 1-2-3 which mathematical operation you want to perform—in this case, multiplication. You see +B4* in the contents box and in the cell.

5. **Point to cell C4 and click the left mouse button.**

   This step selects cell C4, the second cell that you want to include. You see +B4*C4 in the contents box and in the current cell.

after

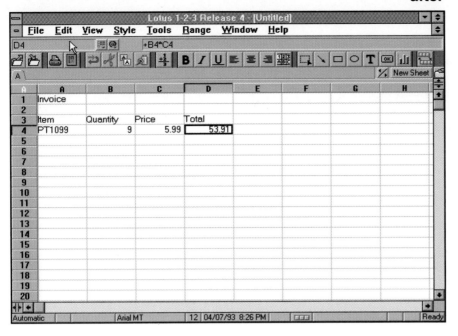

6. Press **Enter**.

Pressing Enter tells 1-2-3 that you are finished with the formula. You see the result of the formula in the cell. The contents box displays the formula—not the result.

1. Click on the cell that you want to enter the multiplication formula into.

2. Press +.

3. Select the first cell you want to include.

4. Press *.

5. Select the second cell you want to include.

6. Continue pressing the operator (*) and selecting cells until you include all the cells you want.

7. Press **Enter**.

To multiply cells

Why use a formula?

You could just type values into the formula, but then if you change the cell contents, the formula will be incorrect. Because the formula references the cells that contain values, the formula changes when you change the values in the cells.

Divide two cells

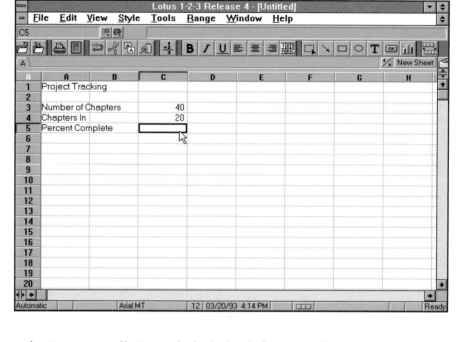

1. **Point to cell C5 and click the left mouse button.**

   This step makes C5 the current cell. This cell is where you want to place the formula.

2. **Press +.**

   This step tells 1-2-3 that you want to enter a formula. The mode indicator changes to Value.

3. **Point to cell C4 and click the left mouse button.**

   This step selects cell C4, the first cell that you want to include in the formula. You see +C4 in the contents box and in the cell.

4. **Press /.**

   The / sign is the operator. It tells 1-2-3 which mathematical operation you want to perform—in this case, division.

5. **Point to cell C3 and click the left mouse button.**

   This step selects cell C3, the second cell that you want to include. You see +C4/C3 in the contents box and in the cell.

6. **Press Enter.**

   Pressing Enter tells 1-2-3 that you are finished with the formula. You see the result of the formula in the cell C5. The contents box displays the formula—not the result.

after

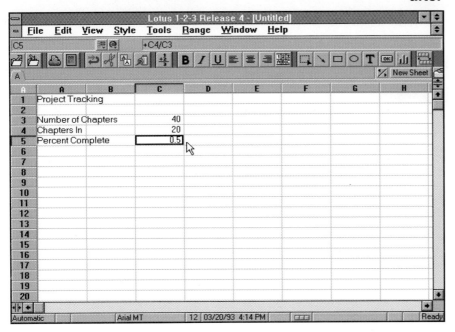

Why use a formula?

You could just type values into the formula, but then if you change the cell contents, the formula will be incorrect. Because the formula references the cells that contain values, the formula changes when you change the values in the cells.

REVIEW

To divide two cells

1. Click on the cell that you want to enter the division formula into.

2. Press +.

3. Select the first cell you want to include.

4. Type /.

5. Select the second cell you want to include.

6. Press **Enter**.

Entering and Editing Data

Overwrite a cell

before

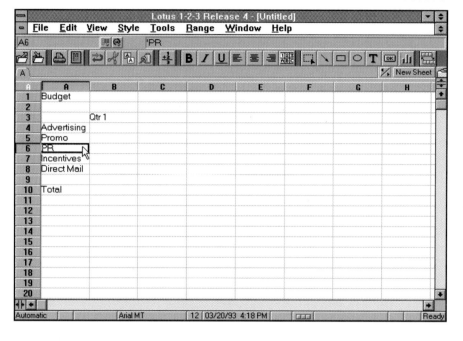

1. **Point to cell A6 and click the left mouse button.**

   This step makes cell A6 the current cell. The contents box displays the current contents of cell A6.

2. **Type Public Relations.**

   Public Relations, the new entry, appears in the contents box and in the cell.

3. **Press Enter.**

   Pressing Enter replaces the previous entry with the new entry.

   Be careful not to overwrite formulas. If you type over a formula and replace it with a value, the result will not be updated if you change other values within the worksheet.

after

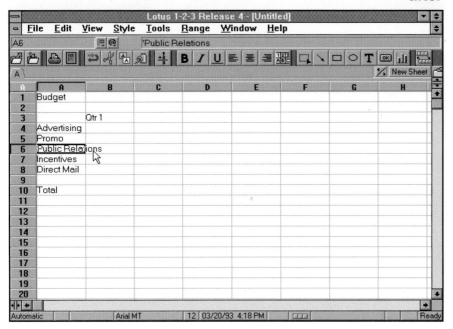

Change your mind?

Before you press Enter, you can press the Esc key to cancel the changes.

REVIEW

1. Click on the cell you want to overwrite.

2. Type the new entry.

3. Press **Enter**.

To overwrite a cell

Edit the cell

If you want to make a minor change to a cell, you can edit the cell's contents. See *TASK: Edit a cell.*

Edit a cell

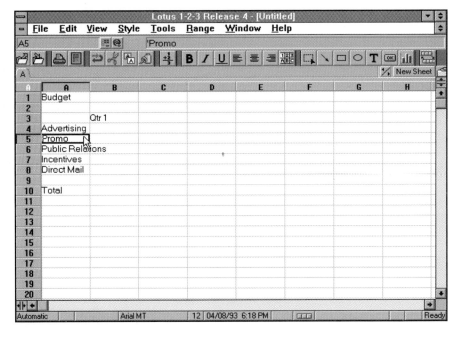

1. **Point to cell A5 and click the left mouse button.**

   This step makes A5 the current cell. This cell contains the entry that you want to change. The mode indicator displays Ready.

2. **Press F2.**

   F2 is the Edit key. Pressing this key allows you to edit the data right in the cell.

   You also can click in the contents box. This step moves the cursor to the contents box; from there you can edit the entry. An X and a check mark appear before the entry. (Clicking on the X cancels the change; clicking on the check mark confirms the new entry.)

   Use the arrow keys to move the cursor to the characters that you want to change or delete. You also can use the Backspace key to delete characters.

3. **Type tions.**

   This entry changes this row label from *Promo* to *Promotions*.

4. **Press Enter.**

   This step accepts the new entry.

after

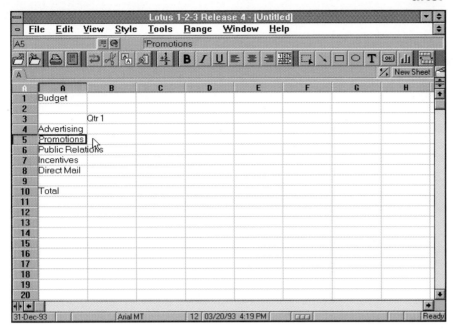

Before you press Enter to accept the entry, you can press the Esc key to cancel any changes.

1. Click on the cell that you want to edit.

2. Press **F2** (Edit).

3. Edit the entry.

4. Press **Enter**.

To edit a cell

Overwrite a cell

If you want to change the entire cell entry, overwrite the entry. See *TASK: Overwrite a cell.*

Erase a cell

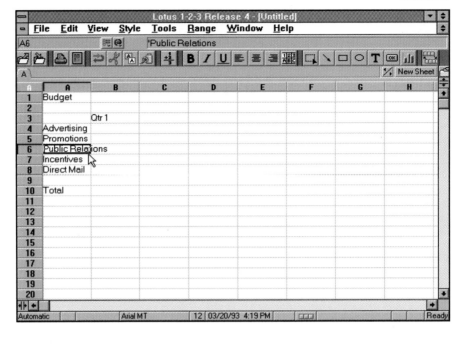

1. **Point to cell A6 and click the left mouse button.**

   This step make A6 the current cell—and the cell that you want to erase. The contents box displays the contents of A6.

2. **Press Del.**

   Pressing the Del key deletes the entry in the cell.

after

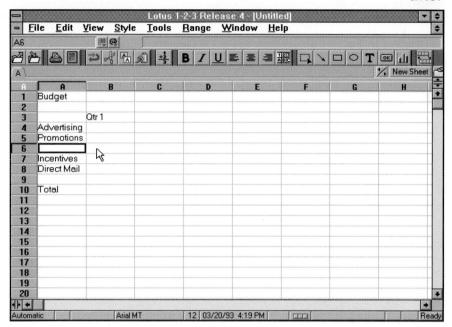

Erase a range

You can also erase a bunch of cells (called a *range*). See *TASK: Delete a range*.

1. Click on the cell you want to erase.

2. Press Del.

To erase a cell

Copy a cell

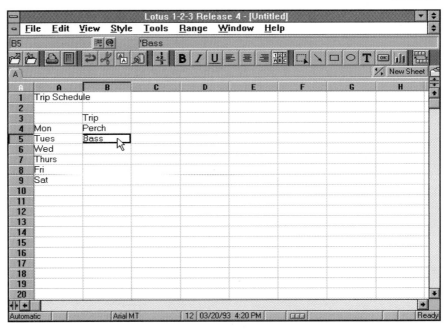

Oops!

To undo the copy, choose the Edit Undo command immediately.

1. **Point to cell B5 and click the left mouse button.**

   This step makes cell B5 the current cell. This is the cell that you want to copy.

2. **Point to Edit in the menu bar and click the left mouse button.**

   This step opens the Edit menu. You see a list of Edit commands.

3. **Point to Copy and click the left mouse button.**

   This step chooses the Copy command.

4. **Point to cell B6 and click the left mouse button.**

   This step makes B6 the current cell. You want the copy to appear in cell B6.

5. **Point to Edit in the menu bar and click the left mouse button.**

   This step opens the Edit menu. You see a list of Edit commands.

after

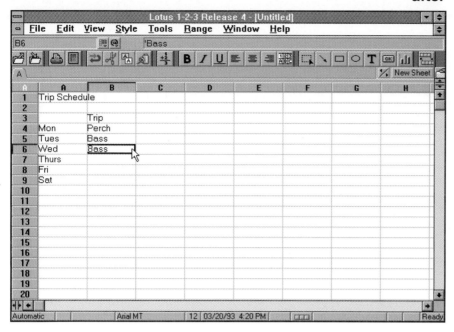

6. Point to **Paste** and click the left mouse button.

This step chooses the Paste command. The entry appears in both cells: B5 and B6. Note that 1-2-3 copies the entry as well as the format (alignment, protection settings, and so on). If you want to learn more about these settings, see the section on formatting the worksheet.

1. Click on the cell that you want to copy.

2. Click on **Edit** in the menu bar.

3. Click on the **Copy** command.

4. Click on the cell that you want the copy to appear in.

5. Click on **Edit** in the menu bar.

6. Click on the **Paste** command.

Copy a range

You can also copy more than one cell (called a *range*). See *TASK: Copy a range.*

To copy a cell

Try a shortcut

Press the Ctrl+C key combination to choose the Edit Copy command. Press the Ctrl+V key combination to choose the Paste command. You also can use the Copy and Paste SmartIcons.

Entering and Editing Data

53

Move a cell

before

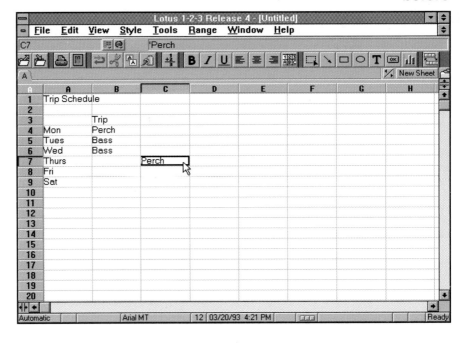

Oops!

To undo the move, immediately choose Edit Undo.

1. **Point to cell C7 and click the mouse button.**

   This step makes C7 the current cell; this is the cell that you want to move.

2. **Point to Edit in the menu bar and click the left mouse button.**

   This step opens the Edit menu. You see a list of Edit commands.

3. **Point to Cut and click the left mouse button.**

   This step chooses the Cut command. The entry is removed from cell C7.

4. **Point to cell B7 and click the left mouse button.**

   This step makes cell B7 the current cell. This is the location where you want the entry to reappear.

5. **Point to Edit in the menu bar and click the left mouse button.**

   This step opens the Edit menu. You see a list of Edit commands.

6. **Point to Paste and click the left mouse button.**

   This step chooses the Paste command. The entry is cut from the original location and pasted to the new location.

Easy 1-2-3 for Windows

after

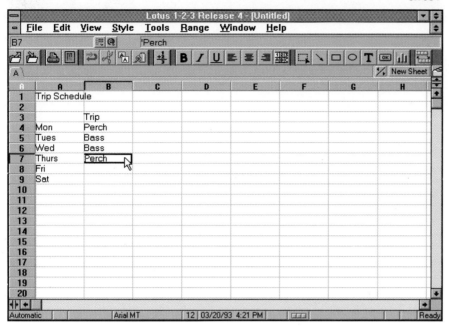

Move a range

You also can move a bunch of cells (called a *range*). See *TASK: Move a range.*

1. Click on the cell that you want to move.

2. Click on **Edit** in the menu bar.

3. Click on the **Cut** command.

4. Click on the cell in which you want the entry to reappear.

5. Click on **Edit** in the menu bar.

6. Click on the **Paste** command.

To move a cell

Try a shortcut

Press the Ctrl+X key combination to choose the Edit Cut command. Press the Ctrl+V key combination to choose the Paste command. You also can use the Cut and Paste SmartIcons.

Go to a specific cell

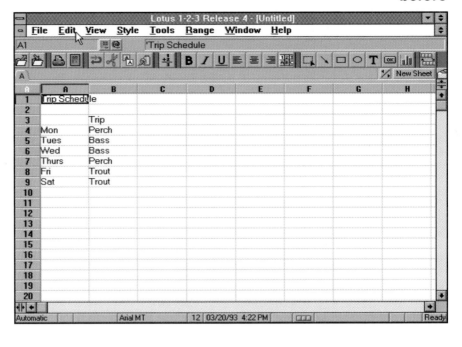

Oops!

To return to the first cell in the worksheet, press the Home key.

1. **Point to Edit in the menu bar and click the left mouse button.**

   This step opens the Edit menu. You see a list of Edit commands.

2. **Point to Go To and click the left mouse button.**

   This step chooses the Go To command. You see the Go To dialog box.

3. **Type B8.**

   B8 is the cell you want to go to. Remember that cells are referenced by the column letter and row number.

4. **Point to OK and click the left mouse button.**

   This step affirms your choice. The cell pointer moves to B8.

after

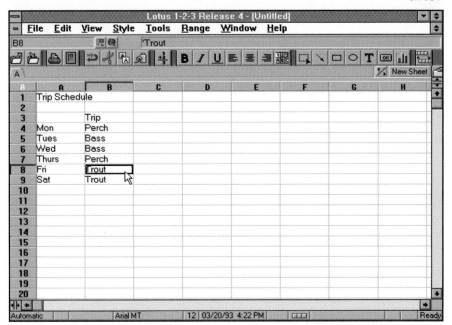

Try a shortcut

Press the F5 key to choose the Go To command.

1. Click on **Edit** in the menu bar.

2. Click on the **Go To** command.

3. Type the cell reference.

4. Click on **OK**.

To go to a specific cell

TASK

Use undo

before

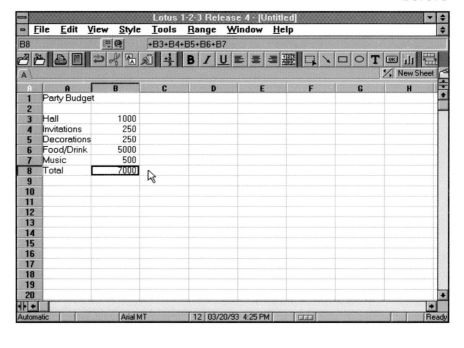

Oops!

If the Undo command is gray, you can't undo the task.

1. **Point to cell B8 and click the left mouse button.**

   You see the current entry in the contents box. Note that this entry is a formula.

2. **Type 9 and press Enter.**

   This step overwrites the formula. But you don't want to overwrite formulas. If you do, the figures may not be correct if the formula has been deleted. You therefore want to undo this change.

3. **Point to Edit in the menu bar and click the left mouse button.**

   This step opens the Edit menu. You see a list of menu commands.

4. **Point to Undo and click the left mouse button.**

   This step chooses the Undo command. The cell is returned to its original form. Notice that the Before and After figures are identical, except for the location of the cell pointer.

Easy 1-2-3 for Windows

after

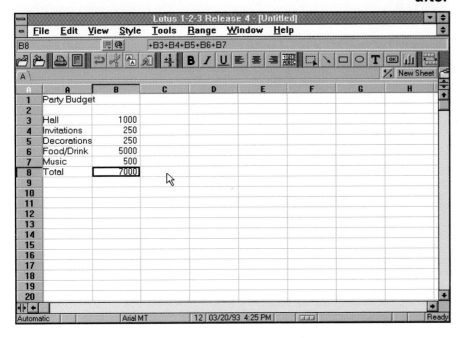

You must choose the Edit Undo command *immediately* after the action that you want to undo. Undo always undoes the last operation. Also, you can undo only certain tasks. Basically you can undo any changes made to worksheet entries—deleting entries, moving entries, copying entries, and so on. See your 1-2-3 for Windows manual or *Using 1-2-3 Release 4.0 for Windows,* Special Edition, for more information.

1. Click on **Edit** in the menu bar.

2. Click on the **Undo** command.

Can't undo the undo

You cannot undo the Undo command.

R E V I E W

To use undo

Try a shortcut

Press the Ctrl+Z key combination to choose the Undo command.

Select a range

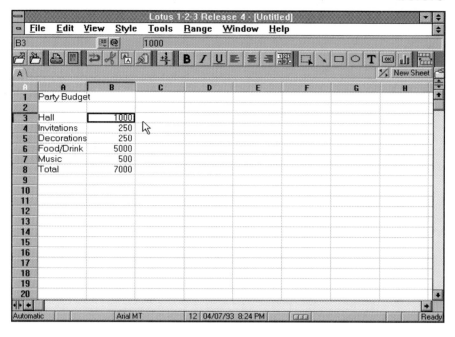

1. **Point to cell B3 and click the left mouse button.**

   B3 is the first cell in the range that you want to select.

2. **Hold down the mouse button and drag down the column until you select the cells B4, B5, B6, B7, and B8.**

   This step selects the range B3..B8. While you drag the mouse, you see the range addresses (coordinates) in the selection indicator.

3. **Release the mouse button.**

   The range is selected. There's a border around the range, and the cells—except for the current cell—appear in reverse video. (The current cell is still white.) You can now copy, cut, move, format, and do other things to the selected range.

after

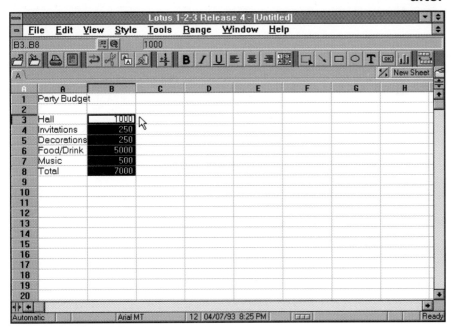

To select a range by using the keyboard, point to the first cell, hold down the Shift key, and use the arrow keys to highlight the range.

REVIEW

1. Click on the first cell that you want to include.

2. Hold down the left mouse button and drag across the cells you want to select.

3. Release the mouse button.

To select a range

Try these shortcuts

To select an entire row, click on the row number. To select an entire column, click on the column letter. To select the entire worksheet, click on the small area above the row numbers and to the left of the column letters.

Managing Files

This section includes the following tasks:

Save a worksheet for
the first time

Save a worksheet
again

Save a worksheet
with a new name

Save a file with
a password

Close a worksheet

Save a worksheet in a
different directory

Save a worksheet on
a different drive

Abandon a worksheet

Open a worksheet

Create a new
worksheet

Open a worksheet in
a different directory

Open a worksheet on
a different drive

Open two worksheets

Switch among open
worksheets

Display more than
one worksheet

Add a sheet to the
worksheet file

Move among sheets

Delete a sheet

Save a worksheet for the first time

```
 ═                    Lotus 1-2-3 Release 4 - [Untitled]              ▼ ▲
 ═  File  Edit  View  Style  Tools  Range  Window  Help                 ▲
 A1              ₩ @        'Division 1
 ☐ ☐ ☐ ☐ ☐ ☐ ☐ ☐ ╬ ┃ B  I  U ≡ ≡ ≡ ▦ ☐ ＼ ☐ ○ T ☒ ╥ ▦
 A                                                          ✕ New Sheet
   ┃    A    ┃   B   ┃   C   ┃   D   ┃   E   ┃   F   ┃   G   ┃   H   ┃ ▲
  1 ┃Division 1┃      ┃       ┃       ┃       ┃       ┃       ┃       ┃
  2 ┃         ┃       ┃       ┃       ┃       ┃       ┃       ┃       ┃
  3 ┃         ┃Qtr 1  ┃Qtr 2  ┃Qtr 3  ┃Qtr 4  ┃       ┃       ┃       ┃
  4 ┃Baseball ┃  350  ┃  325  ┃  300  ┃  325  ┃       ┃       ┃       ┃
  5 ┃Football ┃  450  ┃  425  ┃  400  ┃  500  ┃       ┃       ┃       ┃
  6 ┃Basketball┃ 475  ┃  525  ┃  500  ┃  550  ┃       ┃       ┃       ┃
  7 ┃Soccer   ┃  250  ┃  300  ┃  350  ┃  350  ┃       ┃       ┃       ┃
  8 ┃         ┃       ┃       ┃       ┃       ┃       ┃       ┃       ┃
  9 ┃Total    ┃ 1525  ┃ 1575  ┃ 1550  ┃ 1725  ┃       ┃       ┃       ┃
 10 ┃         ┃       ┃       ┃       ┃       ┃       ┃       ┃       ┃
 11 ┃         ┃       ┃       ┃       ┃       ┃       ┃       ┃       ┃
 12 ┃         ┃       ┃       ┃       ┃       ┃       ┃       ┃       ┃
 13 ┃         ┃       ┃       ┃       ┃       ┃       ┃       ┃       ┃
 14 ┃         ┃       ┃       ┃       ┃       ┃       ┃       ┃       ┃
 15 ┃         ┃       ┃       ┃       ┃       ┃       ┃       ┃       ┃
 16 ┃         ┃       ┃       ┃       ┃       ┃       ┃       ┃       ┃
 17 ┃         ┃       ┃       ┃       ┃       ┃       ┃       ┃       ┃
 18 ┃         ┃       ┃       ┃       ┃       ┃       ┃       ┃       ┃
 19 ┃         ┃       ┃       ┃       ┃       ┃       ┃       ┃       ┃
 20 ┃         ┃       ┃       ┃       ┃       ┃       ┃       ┃       ┃ ▼
 ◄│►│←│                                                           │►│
 Automatic      ┃ Arial MT   ┃ 12 │ 03/20/93 4:29 PM │ ▭▭▭ ┃       Ready
```

Oops!

Click on Cancel for step 4 if you change your mind and don't want to save the worksheet.

1. **Click on File in the menu bar.**

   This step opens the File menu. You see a list of File commands.

2. **Click on Save.**

   This step chooses the Save command. You see the Save As dialog box the first time you save a file. This dialog box lets you name the worksheet. This dialog box includes a file list, a directory list, and a drive list. The insertion point is positioned in the File name text box, and the default name (FILE followed by a number) is listed and selected in this text box.

3. **Type SALEDIV1.**

   This step assigns a file name. You can type up to 8 characters. As a general rule, use only alphanumeric characters. You do not have to type an extension. 1-2-3 automatically adds the WK4 extension.

4. **Click on OK.**

   You return to the worksheet. In the title bar, you see the file name, SALEDIV1.WK4.

after

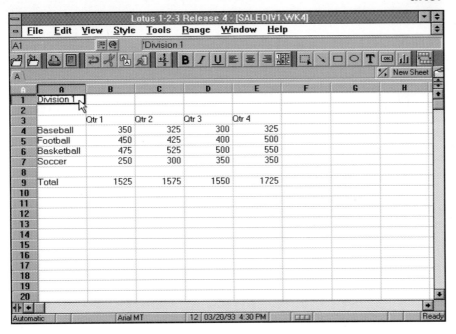

Until you save the worksheet, all of the data is not committed to disk. You can lose the data if something happens, such as a power loss. To be safe, save your work often.

REVIEW

1. Click on **File** in the menu bar.

2. Click on the **Save** command.

3. Type the file name.

4. Click on **OK**.

To save a worksheet for the first time

Try these shortcuts

Press the Ctrl+S key combination to choose the Save command. Or click on the Save SmartIcon.

Save a worksheet again

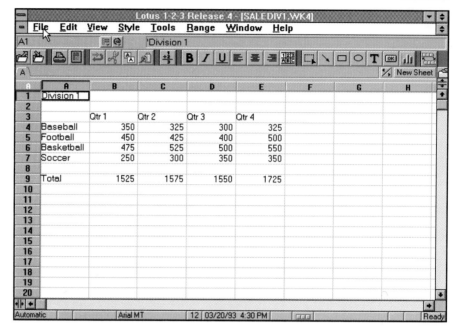

1. **Click on File in the menu bar.**

   This step opens the File menu. You see a list of File commands.

2. **Click on Save.**

   This step chooses the Save command. The file is saved with the same name automatically.

   Note that the Before and After screens for this task look the same.

after

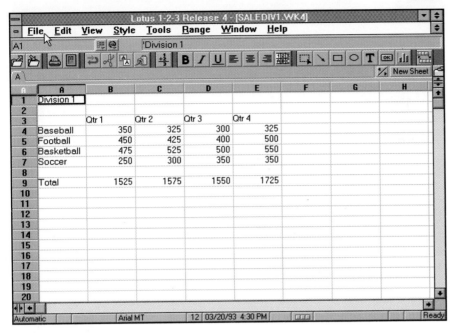

1. Click on **File** in the menu bar.

2. Click on the **Save** command.

REVIEW

To save a worksheet again

If the file has the name FILE000x

If you don't type a name the first time you save the file, 1-2-3 uses the name FILE000*x*, where *x* is the sequence number. If this happens, save the file with a new name. See *TASK: Save a worksheet with a new name.*

Try these shortcuts

Press the Ctrl+S key combination or click the File Save icon to save the file quickly.

Save a worksheet with a new name

before

```
  Lotus 1-2-3 Release 4 - [SALEDIV1.WK4]
 File  Edit  View  Style  Tools  Range  Window  Help
A1                    'Division 2
```

	A	B	C	D	E	F	G	H
1	Division 2							
2								
3		Qtr 1	Qtr 2	Qtr 3	Qtr 4			
4	Baseball	450	350	400	525			
5	Football	450	425	400	500			
6	Basketball	775	525	500	650			
7	Soccer	250	500	450	350			
8								
9	Total	1925	1800	1750	2025			
10								
11								
12								
13								
14								
15								
16								
17								
18								
19								
20								

```
Automatic          Arial MT        12  03/20/93  4:31 PM                    Ready
```

Oops!

If you don't want two copies of the same worksheet, click on Cancel for step 4.

1. Click on **File** in the menu bar.

   This step opens the File menu. You see a list of File commands.

2. Click on **Save As**.

   This step chooses the Save As command. This command enables you to specify a different name for the file. The Save As dialog box appears, and the insertion point is positioned in the File name text box. The current name is listed in this text box.

3. Type **SALEDIV2**.

   This step assigns a new file name. You can type up to 8 characters for the file name. As a general rule, use only alphanumeric characters (letters and numbers). You do not have to type an extension; 1-2-3 automatically adds the WK4 extension.

4. Click on **OK**.

   This step confirms the save and returns you to the worksheet. You see the new file name in the title bar. The original worksheet remains on disk, intact.

after

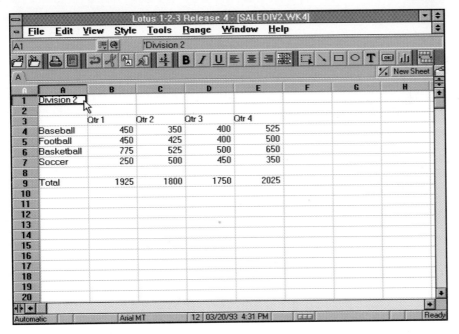

Used the name of another file?

If you type the name of another file, you see an alert box that tells you the file already exists. Click on No and use a different name.

REVIEW

1. Click on **File** in the menu bar.

2. Click on the **Save As** command.

3. Type the new file name.

4. Click on **OK**.

To save a worksheet with a new name

Managing Files

Save a file with a password

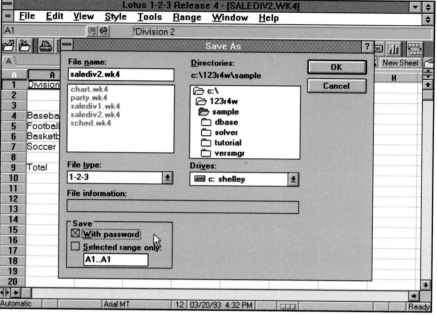

Oops!

To delete the password protection, choose File Save As. In the dialog box, click in the With password check box so that the X disappears. Then click on OK.

1. **Click on File in the menu bar.**

   This step opens the File menu. You see a list of File commands.

2. **Click on Save As.**

   This step chooses the Save As command. You see the Save As dialog box. At the bottom of the left side of the box, look for Save options.

3. **Click on the With password check box.**

   This step selects this feature and puts an X in the check box. The Before screen shows this step. Be sure that the tip of the mouse pointer is positioned inside the box before you click the mouse button.

4. **Click on OK.**

   This step tells 1-2-3 to save the worksheet with the same name, but with a password. You see an alert box that tells you the file already exists.

5. **Click on Replace.**

   This step tells 1-2-3 to replace the existing worksheet with this new password-protected worksheet. The Set Password dialog box appears.

6. **Type elmer and press Tab.**

   This step specifies the password (*elmer*) for the file. You can type any password that you want. Just be sure that you remember your password!

after

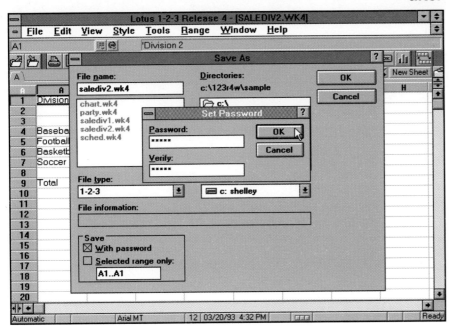

Be careful!

If the worksheet contains particularly sensitive data, don't use a password that's easy to guess. On the other hand, don't use a password that's so complex you forget it!

7. Type **elmer**.

   This step verifies the password. The After screen shows this step.

8. Click on **OK** in the Set Password dialog box.

   This step saves the worksheet. The next time you try to open this worksheet, 1-2-3 will prompt you for the password. Type the password and click on OK.

REVIEW

1. Click on **File** in the menu bar.

2. Click on the **Save As** command.

3. Click on the **With password** check box.

4. Click on **OK**.

5. Click on **Replace**.

6. Type the password and press **Tab**.

7. Type the password again and click on **OK**.

To save a file with a password

Close a worksheet

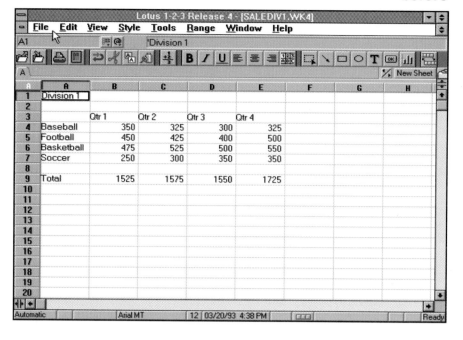

If you didn't save the worksheet before you choose File Close, you see an alert box that reminds you to save the changes. Click on Yes in the alert box. 1-2-3 saves and then closes the worksheet for you.

1. **Save the worksheet.**

   To complete this step, see any of the tasks in this section that discuss saving the worksheet.

2. **Click on File in the menu bar.**

   This step opens the File menu. You see a list of File commands.

3. **Click on Close.**

   This step chooses the Close command. The worksheet closes, and a new, blank worksheet appears on-screen.

after

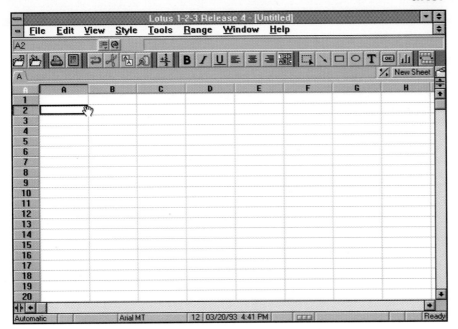

Open the worksheet

Use the File Open command to reopen a closed worksheet. See *TASK: Open a worksheet*.

REVIEW

1. Save the worksheet.

2. Click on **File** in the menu bar.

3. Click on the **Close** command.

To close a worksheet

Save a worksheet in a different directory

before

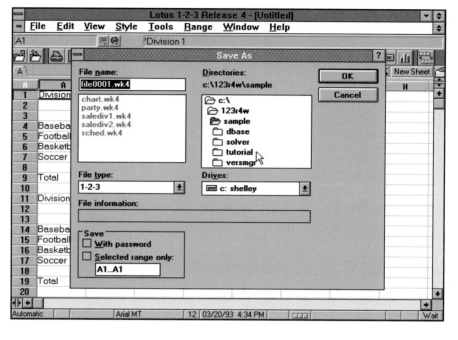

Oops!

If you change your mind and don't want to save the worksheet, click on Cancel for step 6.

1. Click on **File** in the menu bar.

   This step opens the File menu. You see a list of File commands.

2. Click on **Save**.

   This step chooses the Save command. You see the Save As dialog box the first time you save a file. The Before screen shows this step.

   (If you want to save a file that you've already saved to a new location, choose Save As for this step.)

3. Double-click on the **TUTORIAL** directory.

   This step selects this directory and displays the files in that directory. You can tell the directory is selected because its folder icon is shown open. You will save the file to this directory.

4. Click at the beginning of the File name text box; then press the **Backspace** key enough times to delete the contents.

   This step positions the insertion point so that you can begin typing the file name.

5. Type **SALESALL**.

   This step assigns a name to the file you are saving.

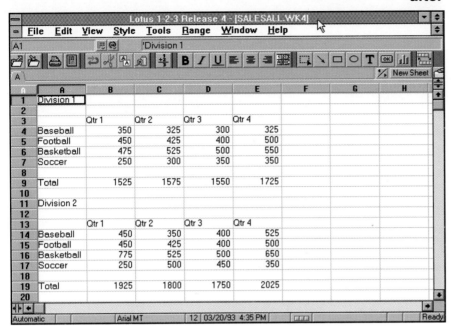

Open the worksheet

See *TASK: Open a worksheet in a different directory* for help on opening the worksheet.

6. Click on **OK**.

   You return to the worksheet. Notice that the file name appears in the title bar.

REVIEW

1. Click on **File** in the menu bar.

2. Click on the **Save** command.

3. In the Save As dialog box, double click on the directory you want to use.

4. Position the insertion point in the file name text box. Make sure that the box is empty.

5. Type the file name.

6. Click on **OK**.

To save a worksheet to a different directory

Save a worksheet on a different drive

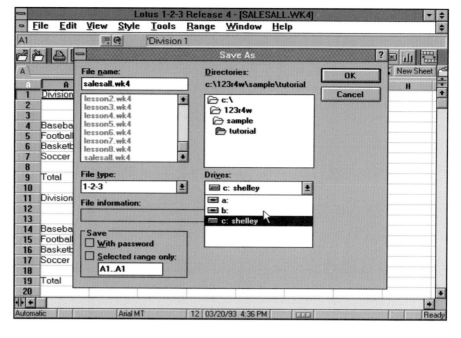

1. Click on **File** in the menu bar.

   This step opens the File menu. You see a list of File commands.

2. Click on **Save As**.

   This step chooses the Save As command. You see the Save As dialog box. The Before screen shows this step.

3. Insert a disk into drive A.

   Drive A is probably the top drive in your computer (if you have two). The disk must be formatted and ready for use. See your DOS manual for help on formatting disks.

4. Click on the down arrow next to the Drives list.

   This step displays a list of drives. The Before screen shows this step.

5. Click on **a:**.

   This step selects drive A and displays the 1-2-3 files on the disk that you inserted into the drive, if there are any files.

after

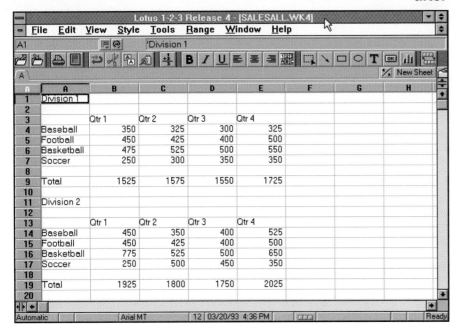

6. Click on **OK**.

This step saves the worksheet with the same name, but a new location: drive A. This procedure is a good way to make a backup copy of your important work. If something happens to the file on your hard drive, you can use the file on the floppy disk.

You return to the worksheet, and the title bar displays the name of the worksheet.

For more information on drives and saving files to them, see *Using 1-2-3 Release 4.0 for Windows,* Special Edition.

Want to know more?

Open a worksheet on another drive

For help opening a worksheet on another drive, see *TASK: Open a worksheet on a different drive.*

REVIEW

1. Click on **File** in the menu bar.
2. Click on the **Save As** command.
3. Insert a disk into the drive.
4. Click on the down arrow next to the Drives list.
5. Click on the drive you want.
6. If you want to use a new file name, type the name.
7. Click on **OK**.

To save a worksheet on a different drive

Abandon a worksheet

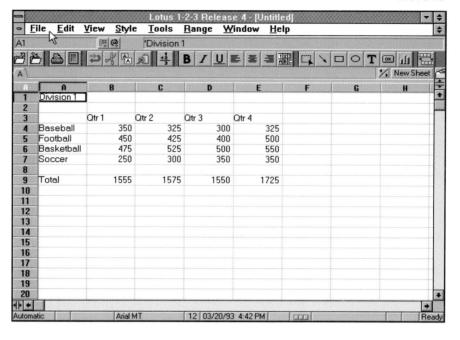

1. **Click on File in the menu bar.**

   This step opens the File menu. You see a list of File commands.

2. **Click on Close.**

   This step chooses the Close command. If you haven't made any changes to the worksheet, the worksheet closes, and you can skip step 3. The Before screen shows this step.

   If you have made changes, you see an alert box that reads Save filename before closing?

3. **Click on No.**

   This step tells 1-2-3 that No, you do not want to save the changes. The worksheet closes, and a blank worksheet appears on-screen.

after

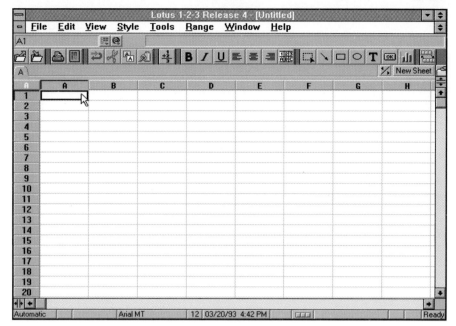

Change your mind?

If you decide that you do need to make changes, click on Cancel in the alert box. 1-2-3 takes you back to the worksheet, where you can make adjustments.

R E V I E W

1. Click on **File** in the menu bar.

2. Click on the **Close** command.

3. Click on **No**.

To abandon a worksheet

Open a worksheet

before

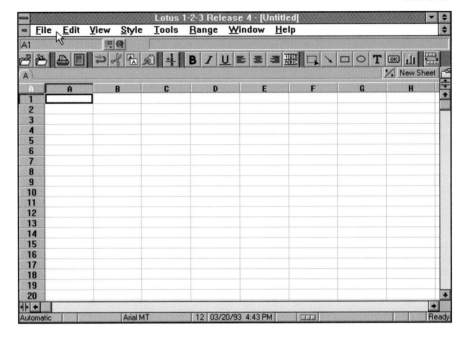

Oops!

If you open the wrong worksheet, close the worksheet and try again.

1. **Click on File in the menu bar.**

   This step opens the File menu. You see a list of File commands.

2. **Click on Open.**

   This step chooses the Open command. You see the Open File dialog box. The insertion point is in the File name text box, and the name *.wk* appears and is selected. This tells 1-2-3 to display only worksheet files. The dialog box also contains a file list, a directory list, and a drive list, among other things.

3. **Type SALEDIV1.**

   SALEDIV1 is the name of the file that you want to open. You don't have to type the extension. You can type the file name if you know it, or you can click on the file name in the Files list.

   If you don't have this file, specify one that you do have.

4. **Click on OK.**

   The worksheet opens and appears on-screen. The file name appears in the title bar.

after

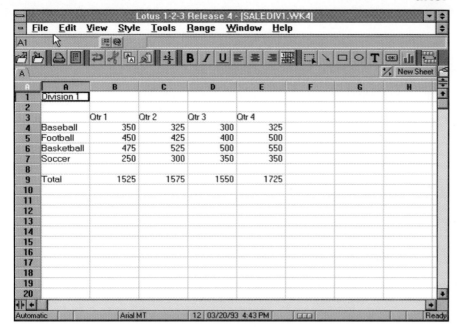

Try these shortcuts

Press the Ctrl+O key combination or click on the File Open SmartIcon to display the Open File dialog box.

To open a worksheet

1. Click on **File** in the menu bar.

2. Click on the **Open** command.

3. Type or select the file name.

4. Click on **OK**.

Select a file quickly

Instead of following steps 3 and 4, double-click on the file name to select and open the worksheet quickly.

Create a new worksheet

before

Lotus 1-2-3 Release 4 - [SALEDIV1.WK4]

	A	B	C	D	E	F	G	H
1	Division 1							
2								
3		Qtr 1	Qtr 2	Qtr 3	Qtr 4			
4	Baseball	350	325	300	325			
5	Football	450	425	400	500			
6	Basketball	475	525	500	550			
7	Soccer	250	300	350	350			
8								
9	Total	1525	1575	1550	1725			

Oops!

If you don't want to create a new worksheet, abandon the worksheet. See *TASK: Abandon a worksheet*.

1. **Save the current worksheet.**

   For help with this step, see any of the tasks on saving in this section. The Before screen shows an open worksheet. If you want, you can close the worksheet (see *TASK: Close a worksheet*).

2. **Click on File in the menu bar.**

   This step selects the File menu. You see a list of File commands.

3. **Click on New.**

   This step chooses the New command. A blank worksheet appears on-screen; the worksheet has the name FILE000*x*, where *x* is the sequence number.

   When you start 1-2-3 and when you close worksheets, a blank worksheet is displayed on-screen automatically.

after

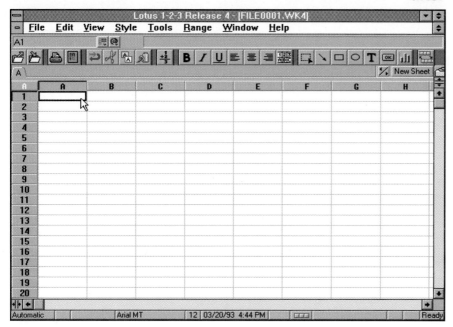

Open several worksheets

You can have several worksheets open at one time. To open several worksheets, see *TASK: Display more than one worksheet.*

1. Click on **File** in the menu bar.

2. Click on the **New** command.

To create a new worksheet

Save the worksheet

Use meaningful names for your worksheets so that you'll remember what they contain. To save this worksheet with a more descriptive name, see *TASK: Save a worksheet with a new name.*

Open a worksheet in a different directory

before

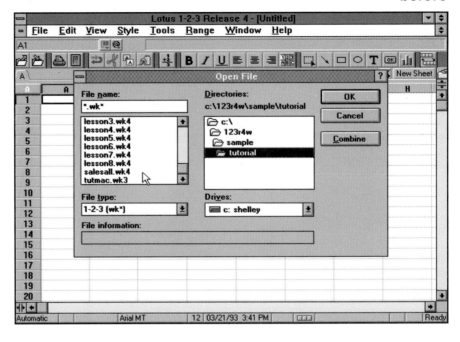

1. **Click on File in the menu bar.**

   This step opens the File menu. You see a list of File commands.

2. **Click on Open.**

   This step chooses the Open command. You see the Open File dialog box.

3. **Double-click on TUTORIAL in the Directories list.**

   This step selects the TUTORIAL directory and displays the files in that directory. You can tell the directory is selected because its folder icon is open. The Before screen shows this step.

4. **Double-click on SALESALL.WK4 in the Files list.**

   This step opens the file. You might have to click on the down-arrow scroll key to scroll the list.

after

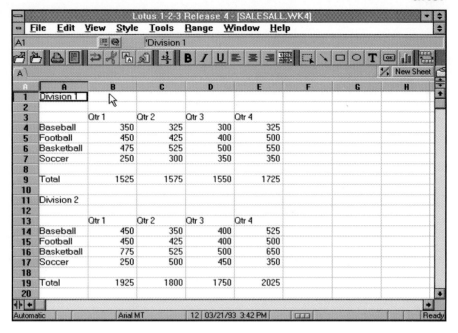

A *directory* is like a manila folder in a filing cabinet. It's an area set aside to store related worksheet or program files. You can have directories within directories (folders within folders).

REVIEW

1. Click on **File** in the menu bar.

2. Click on the **Open** command.

3. Double-click on the directory you want to open.

4. In the Files list, double-click on the file you want to open.

To open a worksheet in a different directory

Want to know more?

To learn more about changing directories, see *Using 1-2-3 Release 4.0 for Windows,* Special Edition.

Open a worksheet on a different drive

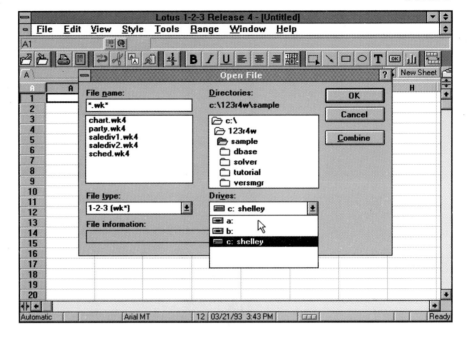

1. Click on **File** in the menu bar.

   This step opens the File menu. You see a list of File commands.

2. Click on **Open**.

   This step chooses the Open command. You see the Open File dialog box.

3. Insert a disk into drive A.

   If you have two floppy disk drives, the top drive is probably A, and the bottom drive is probably B. You can insert a disk into drive B instead of drive A, if you want.

4. Click on the down arrow next to the Drives list.

   This step displays a list of drives, as shown in the Before screen.

5. Click on **a:**.

   This step displays the names of worksheets on this disk. If you inserted the disk in drive B, click on drive B for this step.

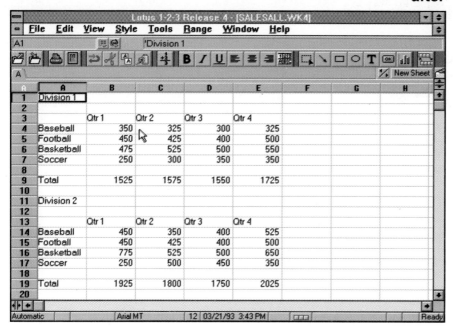

Want to know more?

For more information on changing drives, see *Using 1-2-3 Release 4.0 for Windows,* Special Edition.

6. Double-click on **SALESALL.WK4**.

This step opens the file. You might have to scroll down the File list to find this file.

If you didn't save this file to the disk, this file won't be available. To save this file to the disk, see *TASK: Save a worksheet on a different disk.*

REVIEW

1. Click on **File** in the menu bar.

2. Click on the **Open** command.

3. Click on the down arrow next to the Drives list.

4. Click on the drive letter.

5. Double-click on the name of the file that you want.

To open a worksheet on a different drive

Open two worksheets

before

```
Lotus 1-2-3 Release 4 - [SALEDIV1.WK4]
 File  Edit  View  Style  Tools  Range  Window  Help
A1                      'Division 1
```

	A	B	C	D	E	F	G	H
1	Division 1							
2								
3		Qtr 1	Qtr 2	Qtr 3	Qtr 4			
4	Baseball	350	325	300	325			
5	Football	450	425	400	500			
6	Basketball	475	525	500	550			
7	Soccer	250	300	350	350			
8								
9	Total	1525	1575	1550	1725			
10								

```
Automatic        Arial MT        12  03/21/93  3:44 PM              Ready
```

Oops!

To close a worksheet, see *TASK: Save and close a worksheet* or *TASK: Abandon a worksheet*.

1. **Start with a blank untitled worksheet.**

   For help with this step, see *TASK: Close a worksheet*. You need to close all open worksheets.

2. **Click on File in the menu bar.**

   This step opens the File menu. You see a list of File commands.

3. **Click on Open.**

   This step chooses the Open command. You see the Open File dialog box. The insertion point is positioned in the File name text box. The dialog box also contains file, directory, and drive lists, among other things.

4. **Double-click on SALEDIV1.**

   This step opens the file. The worksheet opens and appears on-screen; notice that the title bar displays the file name. The Before screen shows this step.

   Follow steps 5 through 7 to open another worksheet.

5. **Click on File in the menu bar.**

6. **Click on Open.**

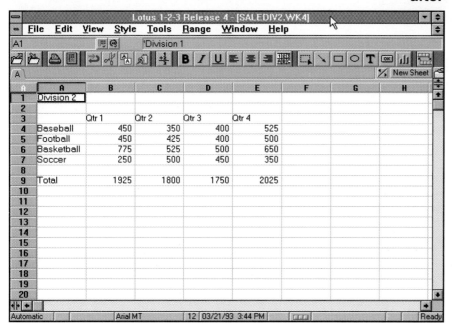

The number of worksheets that you can open depends on how much memory your computer has and how big the files are.

7. Double-click on **SALEDIV2**.

The second worksheet is opened and appears on-screen. This worksheet appears on top of the previously opened worksheet.

REVIEW

1. Click on **File** in the menu bar.

2. Click on the **Open** command.

3. Double-click on the first file name.

4. Click on **File** in the menu bar.

5. Click on the **Open** command.

6. Double-click on the second file name.

To open two worksheets

Try some shortcuts

You can press the Ctrl+O key combination instead of choosing the File Open command. Or you can use the Open File SmartIcon.

Switch among open worksheets

```
─  Lotus 1-2-3 Release 4 - [SALEDIV2.WK4]      ▼ ▲
─  File  Edit  View  Style  Tools  Range  Window  Help    ▲
A1                    ▣ ▣        'Division 1
```

	A	B	C	D	E	F	G	H
1	Division 2							
2								
3		Qtr 1	Qtr 2	Qtr 3	Qtr 4			
4	Baseball	450	350	400	525			
5	Football	450	425	400	500			
6	Basketball	775	525	500	650			
7	Soccer	250	500	450	350			
8								
9	Total	1925	1800	1750	2025			
10								
11								
12								
13								
14								
15								
16								
17								
18								
19								
20								

```
Automatic        Arial MT        12  03/21/93  3:44 PM    ▢▢▢      Ready
```

Oops!

Follow steps 2 and 3 to make the original worksheet active.

1. **Open the SALEDIV1 and SALEDIV2 worksheets.**

   See *TASK: Open two worksheets* if you need help with this step.

2. **Click on Window in the menu bar.**

   This step opens the Window menu. At the bottom of the menu, you see a list of open worksheets.

3. **Click on SALEDIV1.**

   This step selects the SALEDIV1 worksheet. This worksheet moves to the top and becomes the active worksheet.

after

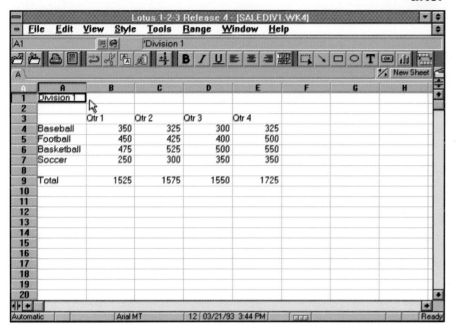

Try this shortcut

If any part of a worksheet is visible on-screen, you can click on that worksheet to make it active.

REVIEW

1. Open the worksheets.

2. Click on **Window**.

3. Click on the name of the worksheet that you want to make active.

To switch among open worksheets

Display more than one worksheet

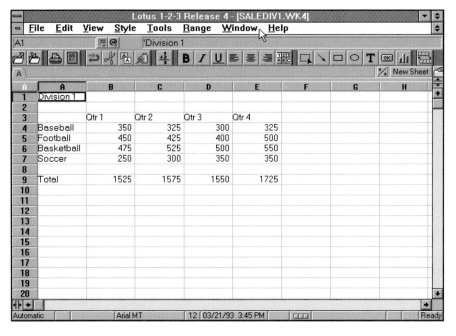

1. **Open the SALEDIV1 and SALEDIV2 worksheets.**

   If you need help with this task, see *TASK: Open two worksheets.*

2. **Click on Window in the menu bar.**

   This step opens the Window menu.

3. **Click on Tile.**

   This step chooses the Tile command. Both worksheets appear on-screen, side by side. The active worksheet is indicated by a darker border.

   You can switch among worksheets by clicking on the one that you want to make active.

Easy 1-2-3 for Windows

after

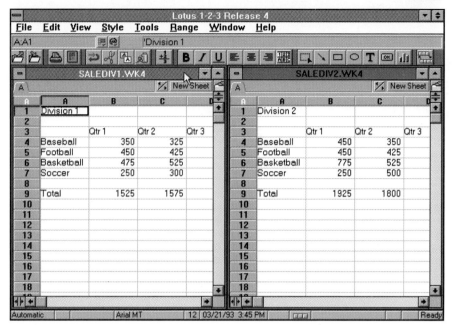

Cascade windows

You also can select Cascade for step 3 to align the worksheets in a different pattern.

1. Open the worksheets that you want to display.

2. Click on **Window** in the menu bar.

3. Click on the **Tile** command.

To display more than one worksheet

Add a sheet to the worksheet file

Oops!

To delete the sheet, see *TASK: Delete a sheet.*

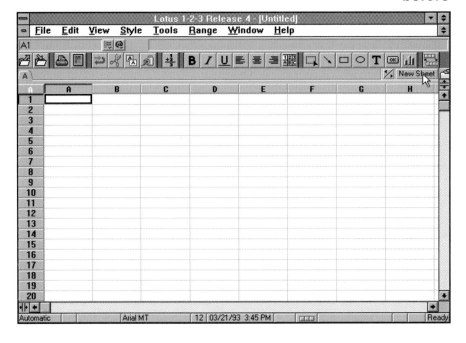

Click on **New Sheet.**

New Sheet is a button on the far right of the worksheet tab line.

This step adds another worksheet to the current file. Each worksheet is indicated with a worksheet tab (A and B in this example). The new sheet is the current one. All data you enter is included in this sheet.

The selection indicator now displays the worksheet letter as part of the cell reference. Also, the worksheet letter appears above the row numbers and to the left of the column letters.

You can enter data the same as you do in any worksheet. When you save the file, all the worksheets are saved. When you open the file, all the worksheets are opened.

after

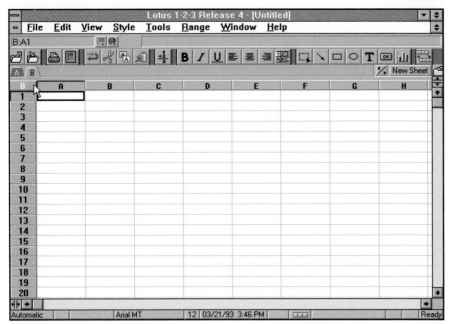

Move among sheets

To move among sheets, see *TASK: Move among sheets*.

Click on **New Sheet**.

To add a sheet to the worksheet file

Why include more than one sheet?

If you have similar worksheets, you might want to store them in the same worksheet file. Use this method. If the worksheets are vastly different and unrelated, store each singular worksheet in its own file. See any of the tasks in this section on saving worksheets.

Move among sheets

before

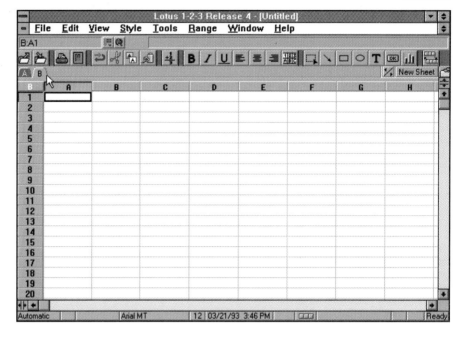

Click on the **A** worksheet tab.

This step makes sheet A active. You can tell which worksheet is active by looking at the tab.

after

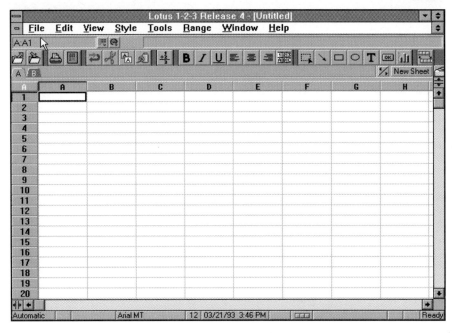

Click on the worksheet tab of the worksheet that you want to make active.

To move among sheets

Delete a sheet

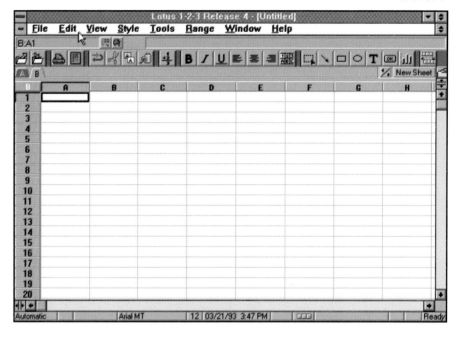

1. Click on the **B** worksheet tab.

   This step selects the sheet that you want to delete. The Before screen shows this step.

2. Click on **Edit** in the menu bar.

   This step opens the Edit menu. You see a list of Edit commands.

3. Click on **Delete**.

   This step chooses the Delete command. The Delete dialog box appears on-screen.

4. Click on **Sheet**.

   This step selects the Sheet option button and indicates to 1-2-3 that you want to delete the selected sheet.

5. Click on **OK**.

   This step affirms that you want to delete the sheet, which 1-2-3 does.

after

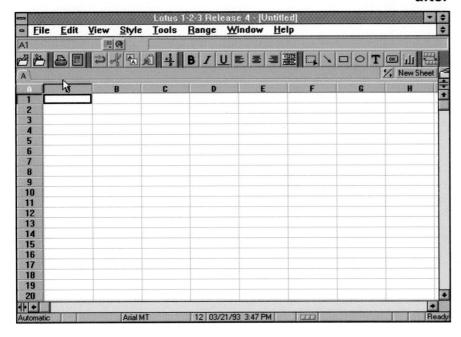

1. Select the sheet that you want to delete.

2. Click on **Edit** in the menu bar.

3. Click on the **Delete** command.

4. Click on the **Sheet** option button.

5. Click on **OK**.

To delete a sheet

Formatting

This section includes the following tasks:

Center a range

Right align a range

Display dollar signs

Display commas

Display percent signs

Format a date

Format a time

Set column width

Insert a row

Insert a column

Delete a row

Delete a column

Hide a column

Center a range

before

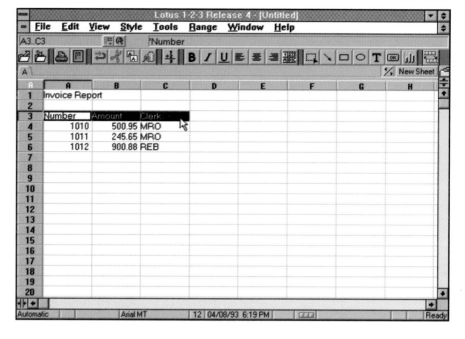

Oops!

To undo the most recent alignment change, choose the Edit Undo command immediately.

1. **Select the range A3..C3.**

   This step selects the range that you want to center. For help with this step, see *TASK: Select a range.*

2. **Click on Style in the menu bar.**

   This step opens the Style menu.

3. **Click on Alignment.**

   This step selects the Alignment command. The Alignment dialog box appears. The selected range is listed in the Range text box.

4. **Click on Center in the Horizontal area.**

   This step selects the Center option button. (The circle or option button should be darkened after you click on it.)

5. **Click on OK.**

   This step confirms the new choice. Each entry in the range is centered in its cell. The range is still selected. A prefix (^) is added to indicate the new alignment.

   The cell is still selected. To deselect it, click on any cell.

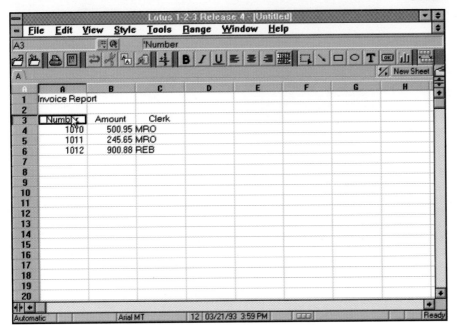

Use a SmartIcon

To center a range quickly, select the range and then click on the Center SmartIcon.

1. Select the range that you want to center.

2. Click on **Style** in the menu bar.

3. Click on the **Alignment** command.

4. Click on the **Center** option button.

5. Click on **OK**.

To center a range

Right align a range

```
┌──────────────────────────────────────────────────────────────┐
│            Lotus 1-2-3 Release 4 - [Untitled]          ▼ ▲    │
│ File  Edit  View  Style  Tools  Range  Window  Help         ▲ │
│ B3.E3                  ┌─┐┌─┐    'Jan                         │
│ [toolbar icons]  B I U ≡ ≡ ≡ 123ABC  ⬚ ╲ ▢ ○ T OK ⅲ ▤       │
│ A ╲                                          ⸝  New Sheet     │
│    A      A       B       C       D       E      F    G   H   │
│  1  Budget                                                    │
│  2                                                            │
│  3        Jan      Feb     March   April                      │
│  4  House     1200    1200    1200    1200                    │
│  5  Utilities  350     325     320     300                    │
│  6  Car        400     400     400     400                    │
│  7  Groceries  250     300     275     325                    │
│  8  Fun        300     500     400     300                    │
│  9                                                            │
│ 10                                                            │
│ 11                                                            │
│ 12                                                            │
│ 13                                                            │
│ 14                                                            │
│ 15                                                            │
│ 16                                                            │
│ 17                                                            │
│ 18                                                            │
│ 19                                                            │
│ 20                                                            │
│ Automatic        Arial MT    12  03/21/93  4:03 PM     Ready  │
└──────────────────────────────────────────────────────────────┘
```

Oops!

To undo the most recent alignment change, immediately choose the Edit Undo command.

1. **Select the range B3..E3.**

   This step selects the range you want to right align. For help with this step, see *TASK: Select a range*.

2. **Click on Style in the menu bar.**

   This step opens the Style menu. You see a list of Style commands.

3. **Click on Alignment.**

   This step chooses the Alignment command. You see the Alignment dialog box. The selected range is listed in the Range text box.

4. **Click on Right in the Horizontal area of the dialog box.**

   This step selects the Right option button. The button should be darkened.

5. **Click on OK.**

   This step confirms the new choice. Each entry in the range is right aligned in its cell. If the entries are text, an alignment prefix (") is added to the entry.

   The range is still selected. To deselect the range, click on any cell.

after

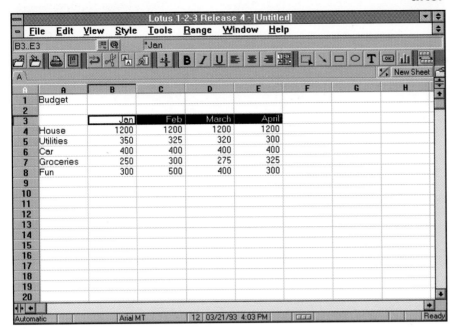

Try a shortcut

Select the range you want to right align, and then click on the Right Align SmartIcon.

REVIEW

1. Select the range that you want to right align.

2. Click on **Style** in the menu bar.

3. Click on the **Alignment** command.

4. Click on the **Right** option button.

5. Click on **OK**.

To right align a range

Display dollar signs

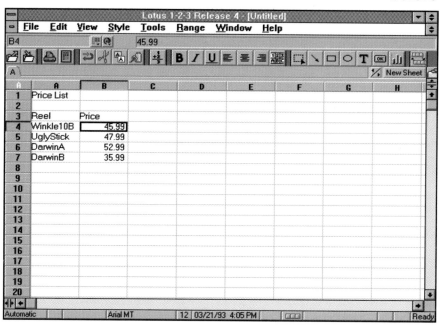

1. **Select the range B4..B7.**

   This step selects the range that you want to change. For help with this step, see *TASK: Select a range.*

2. **Click on Style in the menu bar.**

   This step opens the Style menu. You see a list of Style commands.

3. **Click on Number Format.**

   This step chooses the Number Format command. You see the Number Format dialog box, which lists the available formats.

4. **Click on Currency.**

   This step selects the Currency format. The Decimal places text box displays 2, the default. You might need to scroll through the list to find this option.

5. **Click on OK.**

   This step confirms the choice. The contents box displays the entry as you typed it. But the content in the cell is formatted to show dollar signs and two decimal places. The status bar displays the new format.

   The range is still selected. Click on any cell to deselect the range.

after

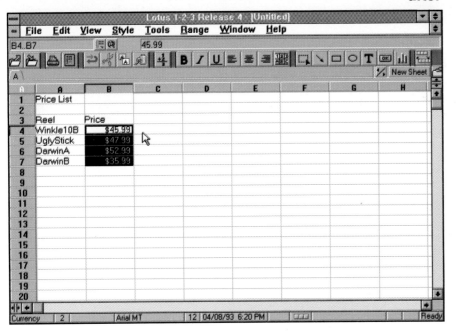

1. Select the range that you want to change.

2. Click on **Style** in the menu bar.

3. Click on the **Number Format** command.

4. Click on **Currency**.

5. If you want, click in the Decimal places text box, delete the default entry, and type the number of decimal places you want displayed.

6. Click on **OK**.

To display dollar signs

See asterisks?

If you see asterisks in the column, the entry is longer than the column and can't fit. You need to change the column width. See *TASK: Set column width.*

Try a shortcut

You can also click on the Number Format panel in the status bar to display a list of number formats. (The Number Format panel is the first panel and usually displays Automatic.) Then click on the number format that you want.

Formatting

107

Display commas

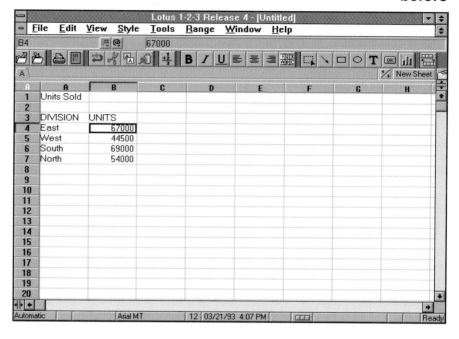

Oops!

To undo the most recent formatting change, immediately choose the Edit Undo command.

1. **Select the range B4..B7.**

   This step selects the range that you want to change. For help with this step, see *TASK: Select a range.*

2. **Click on Style in the menu bar.**

   This step opens the Style menu.

3. **Click on Number Format.**

   This step chooses the Number Format command. You see the Number Format dialog box.

4. **Click on , Comma.**

   This step selects the Comma format.

5. **Click in the Decimal places text box.**

   This step moves the insertion point to the Decimal places text box. The default is two.

6. **Delete the current entry.**

   If the insertion point is in front of the entry, press Del. If the insertion point is after the entry, press Backspace.

7. **Type 0.**

   This step specifies no decimal places.

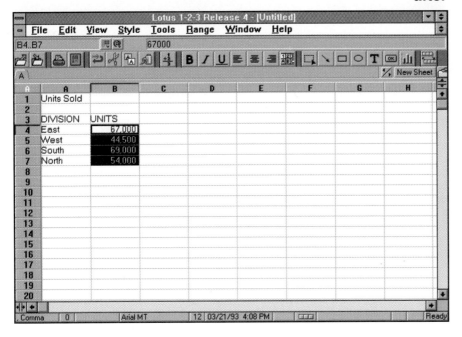

8. Click on **OK**.

   This step confirms the choice. The contents box displays the entry as you typed it, but the content in the cell is formatted to show commas and 0 decimal places. The status bar displays the new format.

   The range is still selected. Click on any cell to deselect the range.

You can also click on the Number Format panel in the status bar to display a list of number formats. Then click on the number format that you want.

Round values

If you select zero decimal places, 1-2-3 rounds the values to fit this format. For instance, if you have 7.5 in a cell and you choose zero decimal places, 1-2-3 displays 8 on-screen. However, the actual value (such as 7.5) will be used in all calculations.

REVIEW

1. Select the range that you want to change.

2. Click on **Style** in the menu bar.

3. Click on the **Number Format** command.

4. Click on **, Comma**.

5. If you want, click in the Decimal places text box, delete the default, and type the number of decimal places you want displayed.

6. Click on **OK**.

To display commas

Display percent signs

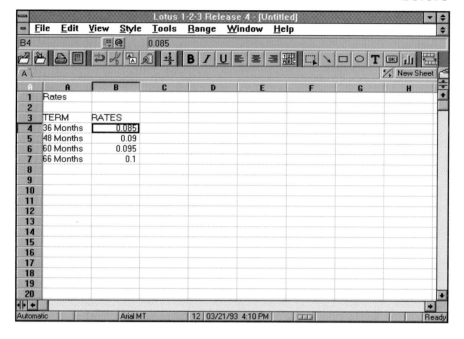

Oops!

To undo the most recent formatting change, immediately choose the Edit Undo command.

1. **Select the range B4..B7.**

   This step selects the range that you want to change. For help with this step, see *TASK: Select a range*.

2. **Click on Style in the menu bar.**

   This step opens the Style menu. You see a list of Style commands.

3. **Click on Number Format.**

   This step chooses the Number Format command. You see the Number Format dialog box.

4. **Click on Percent.**

   This step selects the Percent format.

5. **Click on OK.**

   This step confirms the choice. The contents box displays the entry as you typed it. But the content in the cell is formatted to show percent signs and 2 decimal places. The status bar displays the new format.

   The range is still selected. Click on any cell to deselect the range.

after

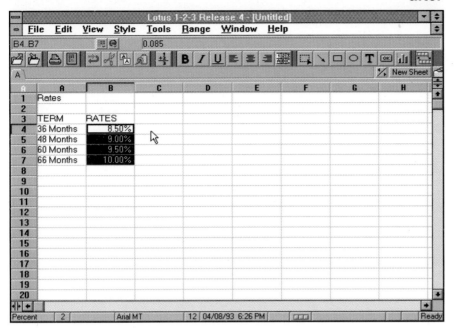

See asterisks?

If you see asterisks in the column, the entry is longer than the column and can't fit. You need to change the column width. See *TASK: Set column width*.

REVIEW

1. Select the range that you want to change.

2. Click on **Style** in the menu bar.

3. Click on the **Number Format** command.

4. Click on **Percent**.

5. If you want, click in the Decimal places text box, delete the default, and type the number of decimal places that you want displayed.

6. Click on **OK**.

To display percent signs

Try a shortcut

You can also click on the Number Format panel in the status bar to display a list of number formats. Then click on the number format that you want.

Format a date

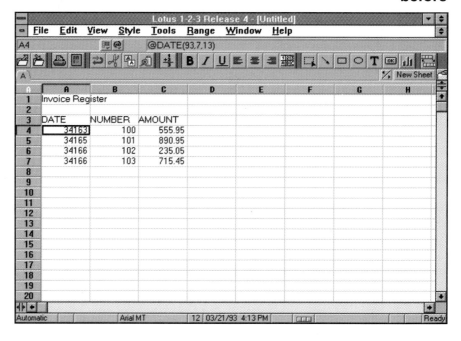

1. **Select the range A4..A7.**

   This step selects the range that you want to change. For help with this step, see *TASK: Select a range*.

   Note that the cells in the range contain date functions. For information on entering dates, see *TASK: Enter a date*.

2. **Click on Style in the menu bar.**

   This step opens the Style menu. You see a list of Style commands.

3. **Click on Number Format.**

   This step chooses the Number Format command. You see the Number Format dialog box.

4. **Click on 31-Dec.**

   This step selects the date format. You probably will have to click on the down scroll arrow in the Format list box to display this format.

5. **Click on OK.**

   This step confirms the choice. The range remains selected. The contents box displays the date function, but dates are displayed in the actual cells.

   The range is still selected. Click on any cell to deselect the range.

Easy 1-2-3 for Windows

after

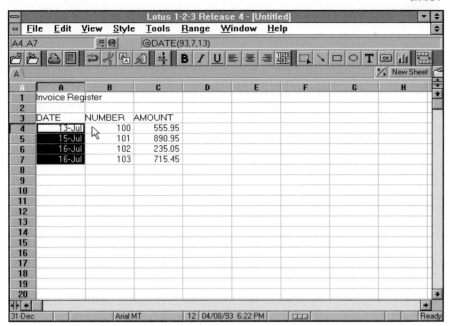

If you see asterisks in the column, the entry is longer than the column and can't fit. You need to change the column width. See *TASK: Set column width.*

REVIEW

1. Select the range you want to change.

2. Click on **Style** in the menu bar.

3. Click on the **Number Format** command.

4. Click on the date format that you want.

5. Click on **OK**.

To format a date

Try a shortcut

You can also click on the Number Format panel in the status bar to display a list of number formats. Then click on the format that you want.

Format a time

before

```
Lotus 1-2-3 Release 4 - [Untitled]
File  Edit  View  Style  Tools  Range  Window  Help
B4                    @TIME(8,0,0)
```

	A	B	C	D	E	F	G	H
1	Trip Schedule							
2								
3		DEPART	ARRIVE					
4	Boat 1	0.333333	0.5					
5	Boat 2	0.333333	0.666667					
6	Boat 3	0.333333	0.666667					

```
Automatic            Arial MT        12  03/21/93  4:17 PM          Ready
```

Oops!

To undo the most recent formatting change, immediately choose the Edit Undo command.

1. **Select the range B4..B6.**

   This step selects the range that you want to change. For help with this step, see *TASK: Select a range*.

   Note that the cells in the range contain time functions. For information on entering times, see *TASK: Enter a time*.

2. **Click on Style in the menu bar.**

   This step opens the Style menu.

3. **Click on Number Format.**

   This step selects the Number Format command. You see the Number Format dialog box.

4. **Click on 11:59 AM.**

   This step selects the time format. You may have to scroll down the Format list to display this one.

5. **Click on OK.**

   This step confirms the choice. The contents box displays the time function, but times are displayed in the actual cells.

   The range is still selected. Click on any cell to deselect the range.

after

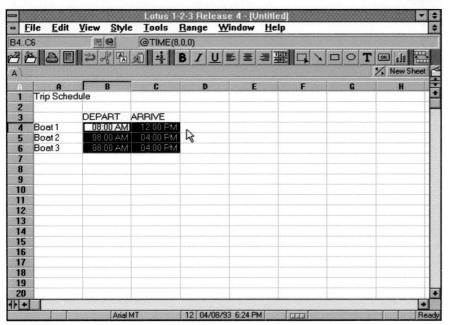

See asterisks

If you see asterisks in the column, the entry is longer than the column and can't fit. You need to change the column width. See *TASK: Set column width.*

REVIEW

1. Select the range that you want to change.

2. Click on **Style** in the menu bar.

3. Click on the **Number Format** command.

4. Click on the time format that you want.

5. Click on **OK**.

To format a time

Try a shortcut

You can also click on the Number Format panel in the status bar to display a list of number formats. Then click on the format that you want.

Set column width

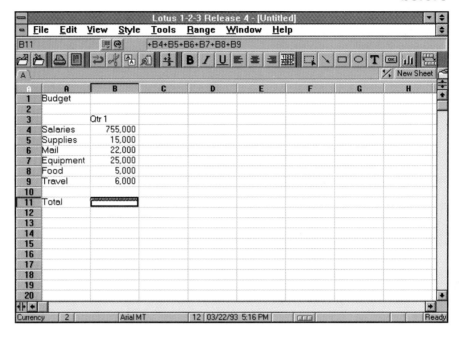

1. **Click on cell B11.**

   This cell currently displays asterisks. When you see asterisks in a cell, the column is not wide enough to display the results. Often formatting makes the entry longer than the default column width. For instance, 828000 is only six characters long, but if you format the number as currency with two decimal places, the number appears as $828,000.00. This entry takes 11 spaces. (For information on formatting, see other tasks in this section.)

   Also, when you enter a number that won't fit in a cell, 1-2-3 uses scientific notation (1.2E+12, for instance) to display that number. In this case, you may also want to widen the column.

   You can select any cell in the column that you want to change.

2. **Click on Style in the menu bar.**

   This step opens the Style menu. You see a list of Style commands.

3. **Click on Column Width.**

   This step selects the Column Width command. You see the Column Width dialog box. The insertion point is positioned in the Set width to characters text box. The default column width, 9 characters, is displayed.

after

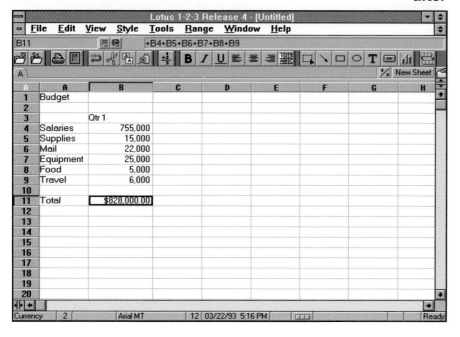

You can easily adjust the column width by using the mouse. Position the mouse pointer on the line to the right of the column you want to widen. Position the mouse pointer where the column letters are located—for instance, between the letters B and C. Hold down the mouse button. Drag the mouse until the column is the size you want, and then release the mouse button.

4. Type **12**.

   This step sets the column width to 12 characters.

5. Click on **OK**.

   The column is widened. If some cells still display asterisks, you need to widen the column even more.

REVIEW

1. Click on any cell in the column you want to change.

2. Click on **Style** in the menu bar.

3. Click on the **Column Width** command.

4. Type the new width.

5. Click on **OK**.

To set column width

Reset width

To reset the width to its original setting, click on the Reset to worksheet default button in the Column Width dialog box.

Insert a row

```
                    Lotus 1-2-3 Release 4 - [Untitled]
  File   Edit   View   Style   Tools   Range   Window   Help
A8..IV8                        105
```

	A	B	C	D	E	F	G	H
1	Check Register							
2								
3	Number	Payee	Amount					
4	100	Altas	$75.99					
5	101	The Gap	$45.88					
6	102	Cash	$25.00					
7	103	Sams	$100.23					
8	105	Shell	$91.21					

```
                    Arial MT        12  03/22/93  5:18 PM              Ready
```

Oops!

To undo the insertion, immediately choose the Edit Undo command.

1. **Click on row number 8.**

   This step selects the entire row. The new row will be inserted above row 8. Be sure to click on the row number—not a cell in the row.

2. **Click on Edit.**

   This step opens the Edit menu. You see a list of Edit commands.

3. **Click on Insert.**

   This step chooses the Insert command. A row is inserted above the current row.

after

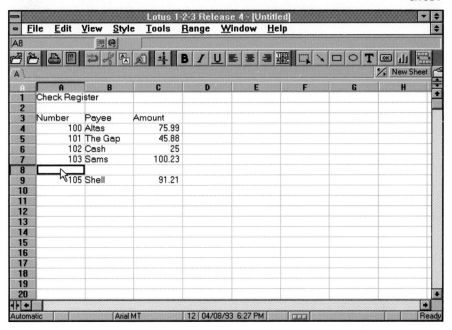

Cell formats are not copied

Note that cell formats are not automatically copied to the new row. You need to format all the columns in the row. For instance, if column C is formatted as currency with two decimal places, you need to format the cell in the new row with this format.

REVIEW

1. Click on a row number. The new row will be inserted above this row.

2. Click on **Edit** in the menu bar.

3. Click on the **Insert** command.

To insert a row

See a dialog box?

If you see the Insert dialog box, you didn't select the entire row. Click on Row in the dialog box, and then click on OK to insert the row.

Insert a column

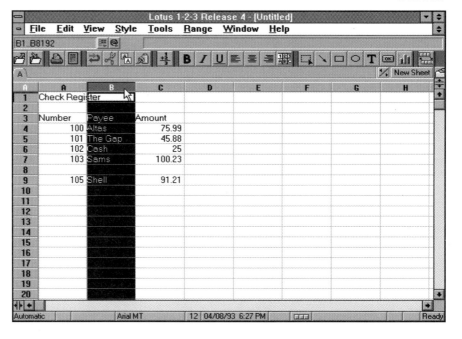

1. **Click on column letter B.**

   This step selects the entire column. The new column will be inserted to the left of column B. Be sure to click on the column letter—not a cell in the column.

2. **Click on Edit in the menu bar.**

   This step opens the Edit menu. You see a list of Edit commands.

3. **Click on Insert.**

   This step chooses the Insert command. 1-2-3 inserts a new column to the left of the current column.

after

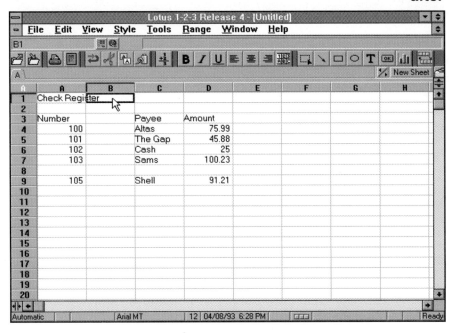

Note that cell formats are not automatically copied to the new column. You need to format all the rows in the column. For instance, if row 4 is formatted as currency, with 2 decimal places, you have to format the cell in the new column with this format.

REVIEW

1. Click on a column letter. The new column will be inserted to the left of this column.

2. Click on **Edit** in the menu bar.

3. Click on the **Insert** command.

To insert a column

See a dialog box?

If you see the Insert dialog box, you didn't select the entire column. Click on Column in the dialog box, and then click on OK to insert the column.

Delete a row

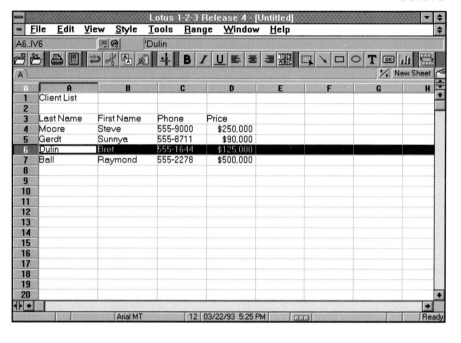

1. Click on row number 6.

   This step selects the entire row. Be sure to click on the row number—not a cell in the row.

2. Click on **Edit** in the menu bar.

   This step opens the Edit menu. You see a list of Edit commands.

3. Click on **Delete**.

   This step chooses the Delete command. The row is deleted. All other rows below that point move up one row.

after

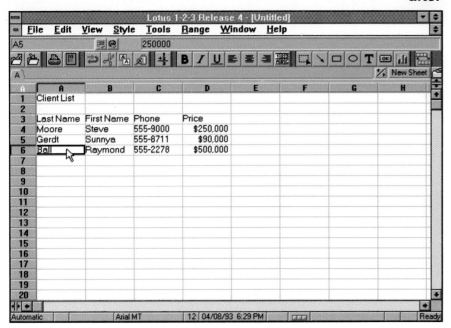

Be careful!

When you delete a row, you delete all the data in that row—including any data that is off screen. Be sure to check the entire row before you delete it.

REVIEW

1. Click on the row number.

2. Click on **Edit** in the menu bar.

3. Click on the **Delete** command.

To delete a row

See a dialog box?

If you see the Delete dialog box, you didn't select the entire row. Click on Row in the dialog box, and then click on OK to delete the row.

Delete a column

before

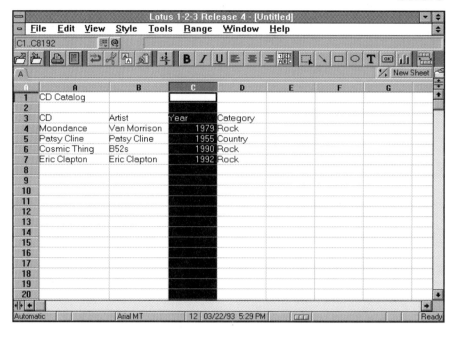

1. **Click on column letter C.**

   This step selects the entire column. Be sure to click on the column letter—not a cell in the column.

2. **Click on Edit in the menu bar.**

   This step opens the Edit menu. You see a list of Edit commands.

3. **Click on Delete.**

   This step selects the Delete command. The column, and all its data, is deleted. All columns to the right of this point move left one column.

after

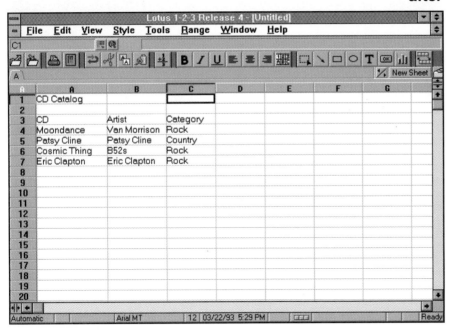

Be careful!

When you delete a column, you delete all the data in that column—including any data that is off screen. Be sure to check the entire column before you delete it.

REVIEW

1. Click on letter of the column that you want to delete.

2. Click on **Edit** in the menu bar.

3. Click on the **Delete** command.

To delete a column

See a dialog box?

If you see the Delete dialog box, you didn't select the entire column. Click on Column in the dialog box, and then click on OK to delete the column.

Formatting

125

Hide a column

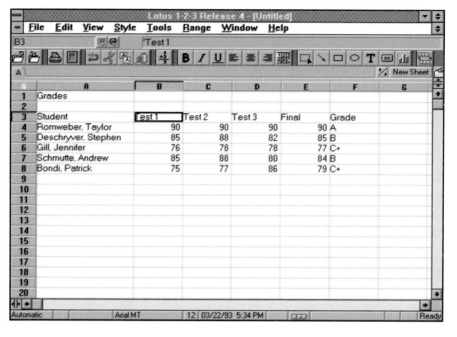

1. **Click on cell B3.**

   Column B is the first column that you want to hide. You can click on any row in the column.

2. **Hold down the mouse button and drag across columns C, D, and E.**

   This step selects columns B, C, D, and E.

3. **Click on Style in the menu bar.**

   This step opens the Style menu. You see a list of Style commands.

4. **Click on Hide.**

   This step chooses the Hide command. You see the Hide dialog box; the Column option button is selected in this dialog box.

5. **Click on OK.**

   This step confirms that you want to hide the columns. The selected columns are hidden. Look at the column order—A, F, G—to verify that the columns have been hidden.

after

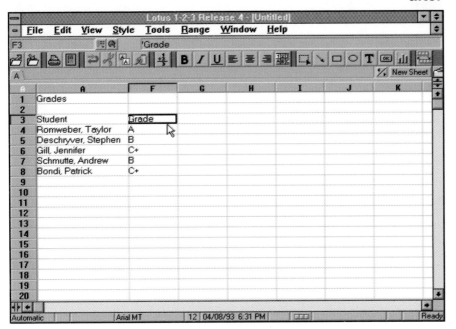

To unhide a column, choose the Style Hide command. In the Range text box, type the cell reference of any cell in the column. Then click on the Show button.

REVIEW

1. Select the column(s) that you want to hide.

2. Click on **Style** in the menu bar.

3. Click on the **Hide** command.

4. Click on **OK**.

To hide a column

More Editing

This section includes the following tasks:

Total cells with the @SUM function

Copy a formula

Copy a range

Delete a range

Move a range

Fill a range

Name a range

Sort data

Replace data

Freeze row titles

Check spelling

Calculate an average

Count items in a list

Figure out a loan payment

Total cells with the @SUM function

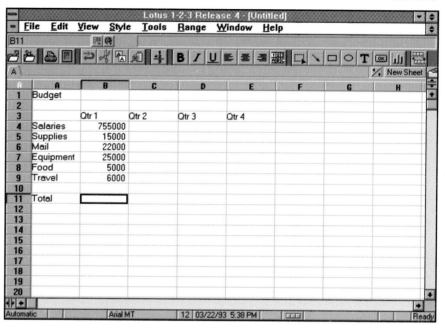

1. **Click on cell B11.**

   B11 is where you want to place the function.

2. **Type @SUM(.**

   @SUM is the name of the function that automatically sums entries in a range. (You can type the function in lowercase or uppercase letters.) You enter the range within the parentheses.

3. **Select the range B4..B10.**

   This step selects the range that you want to sum. The contents box displays @SUM(B4..B10. For help with this step, see *TASK: Select a range*.

4. **Press Enter.**

   Pressing Enter confirms the formula. You see the results of the function in the cell.

   The @SUM function allows you to sum a range. If you later insert or delete rows (or columns) within the range, 1-2-3 automatically updates the total.

after

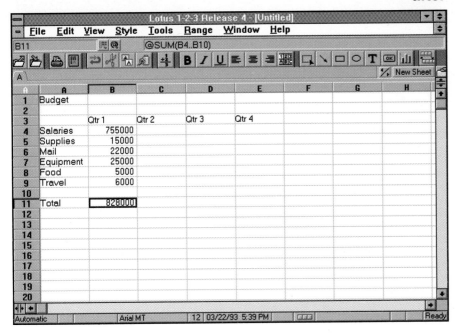

A *function* is a pre-
defined formula. You
provide the different
parts of the formula, and
1-2-3 calculates the
results. 1-2-3 offers
many functions that can
help you with tasks
ranging from figuring
loan payments to
calculating investment
returns. See *Using
1-2-3 Release 4.0 for
Windows,* Special
Edition, for more
information.

REVIEW

1. Click on the cell where you want the sum to appear.

2. Type @SUM(.

3. Select the range you want to sum.

4. Press Enter.

To total cells with the @SUM function

Try a shortcut

Click on the Sum
SmartIcon to sum
cells automatically.

Copy a formula

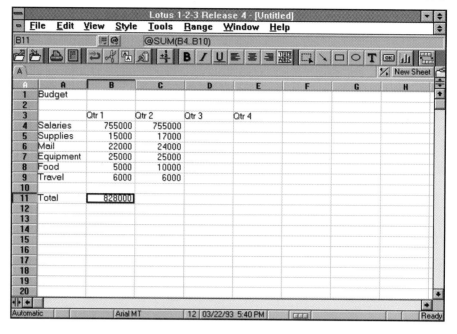

Oops!

To delete the copy, immediately choose the Edit Undo command.

1. **Click on cell B11.**

   B11 contains the formula that you want to copy. (If you have not created this formula, see *TASK: Total cells with the @SUM function.*)

2. **Click on Edit in the menu bar.**

   This step opens the Edit menu. You see a list of Edit commands.

3. **Click on Copy.**

   This step chooses the Copy command.

4. **Click on cell C11.**

   C11 is the cell where you want the copy to appear.

5. **Click on Edit in the menu bar.**

   This step opens the Edit menu.

6. **Click on Paste.**

   This step chooses the Paste command. The formula is pasted into the cell, and the results of the formula appear in cell C11.

after

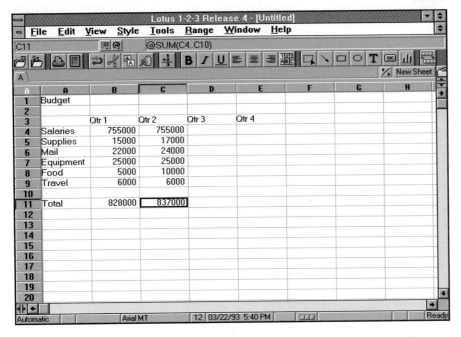

Drag a copy

To copy a cell by dragging, select the cell. Position the mouse pointer on the border of the cell; the mouse pointer changes to a hand. Hold down the Ctrl key and drag the cell to where you want the copy. Then release the Ctrl key and the mouse button.

Note that the contents box contains the formula @SUM(C4..C10). This formula references the current column. This is because of a 1-2-3 concept known as *relative addressing*. 1-2-3 automatically adjusts cell references. For more information on relative addresses, see *Using 1-2-3 Release 4.0 for Windows,* Special Edition.

REVIEW

1. Click on the cell that contains the formula you want to copy.

2. Click on **Edit** in the menu bar.

3. Click on the **Copy** command.

4. Click on the cell where you want the copy to appear.

5. Click on **Edit** in the menu bar.

6. Click on the **Paste** command.

To copy a formula

Try these shortcuts

Press the Ctrl+C key combination to select the Edit Copy command. Press the Ctrl+V key combination to select the Paste command. Or use the Copy and Paste SmartIcons.

TASK

Copy a range

before

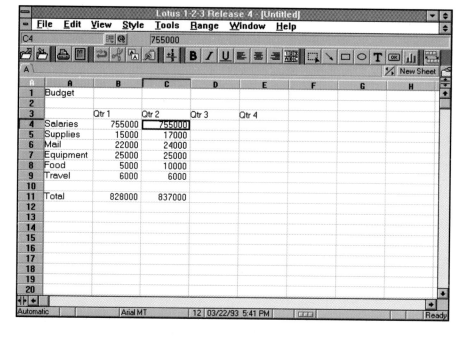

Oops!

To undo the copy,
immediately choose the
Edit Undo command.
Or just delete the
copied range; see
TASK: Delete a range.

1. **Select the range C4..C11.**

   This step selects the range that you want to copy. For help with this step, see *TASK: Select a range.*

2. **Click on Edit in the menu bar.**

   This step opens the Edit menu. You see a list of Edit commands.

3. **Click on Copy.**

   This step chooses the Copy command.

4. **Click on D4.**

   D4 is the first cell where you want to place the copied range. The copied range will take the same shape and space as the original, so you only have to include the first cell in the range to be copied to. Be careful not to overwrite existing data.

5. **Click on Edit in the menu bar.**

   This step opens the Edit menu.

6. **Click on Paste.**

   This step chooses the Paste command. 1-2-3 copies the range to the new location.

after

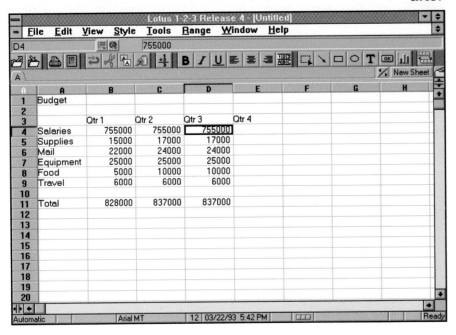

Drag a copy

To copy a range by dragging, select the range. Position the mouse pointer on the border of the range; the mouse pointer changes to a hand. Hold down the Ctrl key and drag the range to where you want the copy. Then release the Ctrl key and the mouse button.

REVIEW

1. Select the range that you want to copy.

2. Click on **Edit** in the menu bar.

3. Click on the **Copy** command.

4. Click on the first cell of the destination—the spot where you want to place the copy of the range.

5. Click on **Edit** in the menu bar.

6. Click on the **Paste** command.

To copy a range

Try these shortcuts

Press the Ctrl+C key combination to select the Edit Copy command. Press the Ctrl+V key combination to select the Paste command. Or use the Copy and Paste SmartIcons.

Delete a range

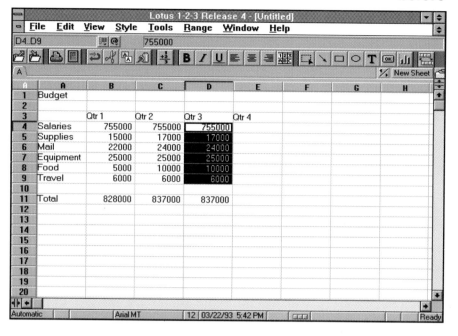

1. **Select the range D4..D9.**

   This step selects the range that you want to delete. For help with this step, see *TASK: Select a range*.

2. **Press Del.**

   Pressing the Del key deletes the range. The column total in cell D11 is adjusted to zero, and the range is still selected. Click on any cell to deselect the range.

after

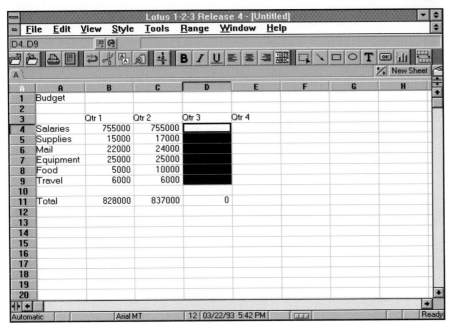

Be careful!

When you erase a range that is included in a formula, the formula is recalculated. Be sure that you don't erase any values that you need for a formula.

REVIEW

1. Select the range you want to delete.

2. Press **Del**.

To delete a range

Move a range

before

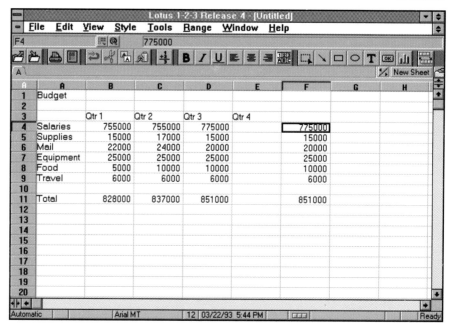

1. **Select the range F4..F11.**

   This step selects the range that you want to move. For help with this step, see *TASK: Select a range.*

2. **Click on Edit in the menu bar.**

   This step opens the Edit menu. You see a list of Edit commands.

3. **Click on Cut.**

   This step chooses the Cut command. The range disappears from the worksheet.

4. **Click on cell E4.**

   E4 is the first cell where you want to place the range. The range will have the same shape and take the same space as the original, so you only have to select the first cell in new location for the range. Be careful not to overwrite existing data.

5. **Click on Edit in the menu bar.**

   This step opens the Edit menu.

6. **Click on Paste.**

   This step chooses the Paste command. The selected range is pasted to the new location.

after

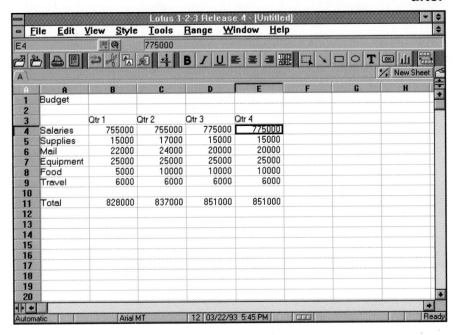

Try these shortcuts

Press the Ctrl+X key combination to select the Cut command. Press the Ctrl+V key combination to select the Paste command. Or use the Cut and Paste SmartIcons.

REVIEW

1. Select the range that you want to move.

2. Click on **Edit** in the menu bar.

3. Click on the **Cut** command.

4. Click on the cell where you want to place the range.

5. Click on **Edit** in the menu bar.

6. Click on the **Paste** command.

To move a range

Drag a range

To drag a range, select it. Then position the pointer along any edge of the range; the pointer changes to the shape of a hand. Hold down the mouse button and drag the range to its new location.

Fill a range

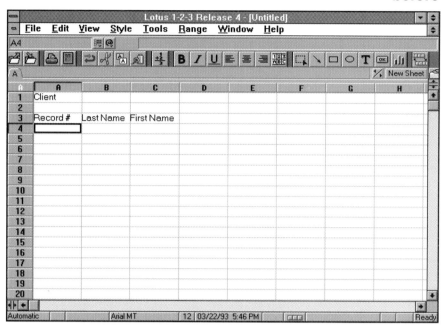

1. **Select the range A4..A15.**

   This step selects the range that you want to fill. For help with this step, see *TASK: Select a range*.

2. **Click on Range in the menu bar.**

   This step opens the Range menu. You see a list of Range commands.

3. **Click on Fill.**

   This step chooses the Fill command. You see the Fill dialog box. Here you specify the start value, the increment, and the stop value. The insertion point is positioned in the Start text box.

4. **Type 1.**

   This step tells 1-2-3 to start the numbering with 1.

5. **Click on OK.**

   This step confirms the other settings. On-screen the range you selected is filled with numbers, starting with 1 and incremented by 1. If you do not specify a stop value, 1-2-3 stops when the selected range is full.

   The range is still selected. Click on any cell to deselect the range.

after

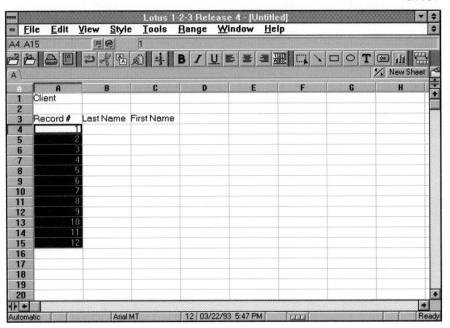

Why fill a range?

Use this procedure when you need to enter a series of numbers—perhaps when you're setting up a checkbook on the computer and want the numbers to represent the check numbers.

REVIEW

1. Select the range you want to fill.

2. Click on **Range** in the menu bar.

3. Click on the **Fill** command.

4. Enter a start value.

5. If you want, also enter an increment value and stop value.

6. Click on **OK**.

To fill a range

More Editing

141

TASK

Name a range

before

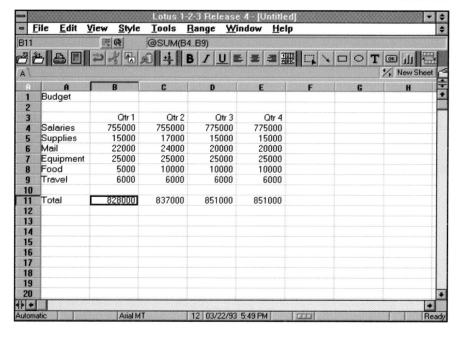

Oops!

To undo the range name, immediately choose the Edit Undo command.

1. **Click on cell B11.**

   B11 is the cell that you want to name.

2. **Click on Range in the menu bar.**

   This step opens the Range menu. You see a list of Range commands.

3. **Click on Name.**

   This steps selects the Name command. The Name dialog box appears, and the insertion point is positioned in the Name text box.

4. **Type QTR1.**

   QTR1 is the name that you want to assign this range. (In this example, the range is only one cell.)

   As a general rule, type up to 15 characters using either uppercase or lowercase letters. Use only alphanumeric characters—letters and numbers. Don't use spaces, don't start the name with a number, and don't use a name that looks like a cell address (B11, for example).

142

Easy 1-2-3 for Windows

after

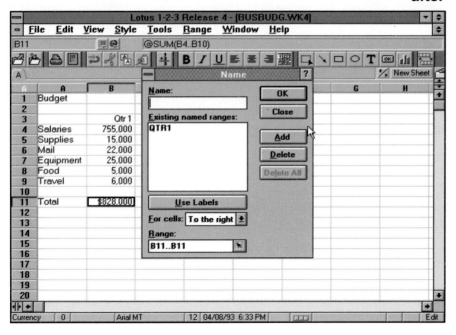

Why name ranges?

Naming ranges offers several advantages. Names are easier to remember than cell addresses. When prompted for a range to move or copy, for instance, you can simply type the name. You also can use range names in formulas. For instance, you can type the formula **+QTR1+QTR2**. Finally, you can use the GoTo key (F5) to move to a named range quickly.

5. Click on **Add**.

   This step chooses the Add command button. 1-2-3 adds the name to the list of existing names. The After screen shows this step.

6. Click on **OK**.

   This step confirms the range name. Nothing on-screen changes. The cell and the contents box look the same. The name is saved with the worksheet when you save the worksheet.

Delete a range name

To delete a range name, choose the Range Name command, select the name from the list of range names, click on Delete, and then click on OK.

REVIEW

1. Select the range that you want to name.

2. Click on **Range** in the menu bar.

3. Click on the **Name** command.

4. Type the name in the Name text box.

5. Click on the **Add** command button.

6. Click on **OK**.

To name a range

More Editing

143

Sort data

Oops!

If the sort did not work as planned, immediately choose the Edit Undo command to restore the range to its original order.

1. **Select the range A4..D7.**

   This step selects the range that you want to sort. Be sure to include the entire range—not just the column you want to sort. If you select just the column, the entries will be mismatched. Also be sure to select just the data; do not include row or column headings.

2. **Click on Range in the menu bar.**

   This step opens the Range menu. You see a list of Range commands.

3. **Click on Sort.**

   This step selects the Sort command. You see the Sort dialog box, which lists the selected range. The current cell is listed in the text box named Sort by.

4. **Click on OK.**

   This step starts the sort. The data is sorted on-screen in alphabetical order by last name.

   You can perform other kinds of sorts. To learn more about your sorting options, see *Using 1-2-3 Release 4.0 for Windows,* Special Edition.

after

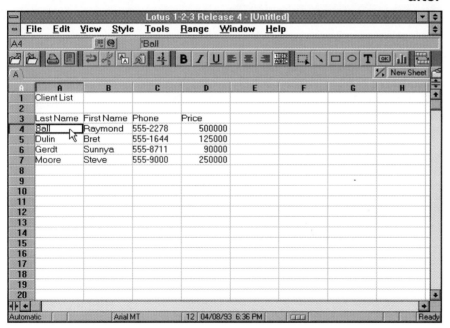

Sort numbers

This example sorts text, but you can use this same procedure to sort numbers.

REVIEW

1. Select the range that you want to sort.

2. Click on **Range** in the menu bar.

3. Click on the **Sort** command.

4. Click on **OK** to accept the default settings. Or change any settings and then click on **OK**.

To sort data

Replace data

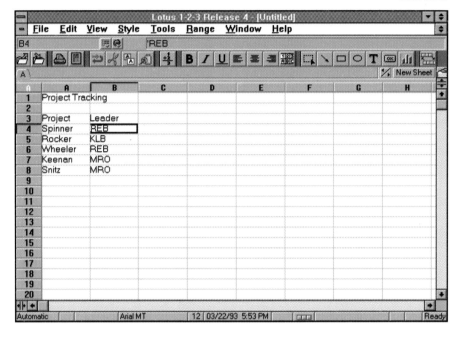

Oops!

To undo the replacements, immediately choose the Edit Undo command.

1. **Select the range B4..B8.**

   This step selects the range that you want to search.

2. **Click on Edit in the menu bar.**

   This step opens the Edit menu.

3. **Click on Find & Replace.**

   This step selects the Find & Replace command. You see the Find & Replace dialog box.

4. **Type REB.**

   REB is the text that you want to search and replace.

5. **In the Action area, click on Replace with.**

   This step selects the Replace with option button.

6. **Type KLB.**

   KLB is the new text—the text you want to use as the replacement.

7. **Click on OK.**

   You now see the Replace dialog box.

8. **Click on Replace All.**

   This step starts the search and tells 1-2-3 to replace all occurrences of the text.

after

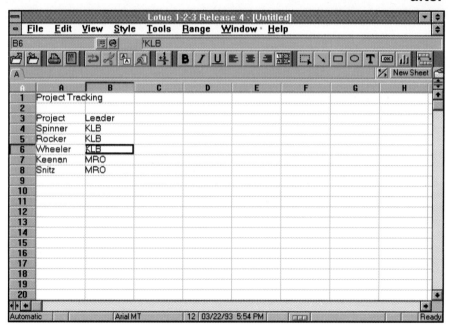

Be careful!

Be sure that you want to replace all occurrences before you select Replace All.

REVIEW

1. Select the range to search.

2. Click on **Edit** in the menu bar.

3. Click on the **Find & Replace** command.

4. Type the search text in the Search for text box.

5. Click on the **Replace with** option button.

6. Type the replacement text in the Replace with text box.

7. Click on **OK**.

8. Click on the **Replace All** command button.

To replace data

Try some other searches

You can search and replace options one occurrence at a time. For complete information about all the search options, see *Using 1-2-3 Release 4.0 for Windows,* Special Edition.

Freeze row titles

```
┌─────────────────────────────────────────────────────────────────────┐
│                Lotus 1-2-3 Release 4 - [Untitled]              ▼  ▲   │
│  File   Edit   View   Style   Tools   Range   Window   Help          ▲│
│ A4              ▦ Q        'Spinner                                   │
│ [toolbar icons]  ½ B  I  U ≡ ≡ ≡ ▦  ▭ \ □ ○ T ▣ ▥ ▦                  │
│ A\                                               ╱ New Sheet          │
│  A       A        B        C       D        E         F       G    H  │
│  1  P&L                                                               │
│  2                                                                    │
│  3  Product   Sales    Returns   Net      % Return   Cost/Unit        │
│  4  Spinner   25,000    2,500    22,500     10%        1.25           │
│  5  Rocker    40,000    3,500    36,500      9%        0.55           │
│  6  Wheeler   50,000    5,500    44,500     11%        1.65           │
│  7  Keenan    60,000    7,000    53,000     12%        3.25           │
│  8  Snitz     30,000    2,500    27,500      8%        2.25           │
│  9                                                                    │
│ 10                                                                    │
│ 11                                                                    │
│ 12                                                                    │
│ 13                                                                    │
│ 14                                                                    │
│ 15                                                                    │
│ 16                                                                    │
│ 17                                                                    │
│ 18                                                                    │
│ 19                                                                    │
│ 20                                                                    │
│ Automatic        Arial MT       12  03/22/93 5:58 PM    ▭▭▭    Ready  │
└─────────────────────────────────────────────────────────────────────┘
```

Oops!

To undo the command, choose the View Clear Titles command.

1. **Click on cell A4.**

   This step tells 1-2-3 where to freeze the titles. All rows above row 4 will be frozen on-screen.

2. **Click on View in the menu bar.**

   This step opens the View menu. You see a list of View commands.

3. **Click on Freeze Titles.**

   This step selects the Freeze Titles command. You see the Freeze Titles dialog box. The Rows options is selected—this is the option that you want.

4. **Click on OK.**

   This step confirms the command. Now when you scroll on-screen, rows 1-3 remain at the top of the spreadsheet.

   The After screen shows the worksheet scrolled. Freezing titles is useful when you have a big worksheet and need to see the row or column headings as you enter data.

after

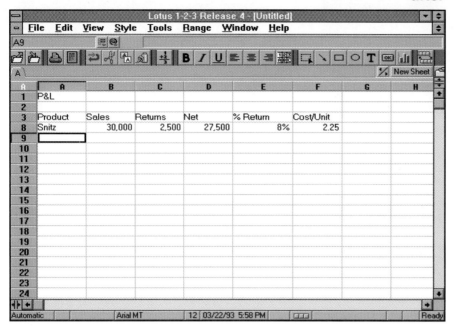

Freeze columns

You also can freeze columns—or both rows and columns. See *Using 1-2-3 Release 4.0 for Windows,* Special Edition, for more information.

REVIEW

1. Select a row. All rows above this row will be frozen on-screen.

2. Click on **View** in the menu bar.

3. Click on the **Freeze Titles** command.

4. Click on **OK**.

To freeze row titles

More Editing

149

Check spelling

1. **Click on Tools in the menu bar.**

   This step opens the Tools menu. You see a list of Tools commands.

2. **Click on Spell Check.**

   This step selects the Spell Check command. You see the Spell Check dialog box. 1-2-3 checks the entire file unless you specify otherwise.

3. **Click on OK.**

   This step starts the spelling check. 1-2-3 compares the words in the worksheet to those in its dictionary and flags any unknown words.

   In this example, the speller stops on *Socceer* and displays a dialog box. It lists the unknown word and alternative spellings.

4. **In the Alternatives list, click on Soccer.**

   This step selects the correct spelling. If the correct spelling isn't listed, you can type it in the Replace with text box.

5. **Click on Replace All.**

   This step replaces all the occurrences of this word with the correct spelling and continues the spelling check. When the spelling check is complete, 1-2-3 displays a dialog box.

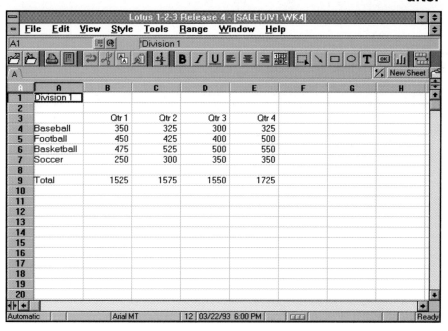

Skip a word

To skip a word, click on Skip in the Spell Check Unknown word dialog box.

6. Click on OK.

To check spelling

1. Click on Tools in the menu bar.

2. Click on the Spell Check command.

3. Click on OK.

4. When 1-2-3 stops on an unknown word, do one of the following:

   • Click on an alternative spelling in the list. Then click on Replace All.

   • Click on Skip or Skip All to skip the word.

   • Click on Add To Dictionary to add the word to the list of words that 1-2-3 recognizes.

5. When the check is complete, click on OK.

Want to know more?

For more information on all spelling check options, see Using *1-2-3 Release 4.0 for Windows*, Special Edition.

Calculate an average

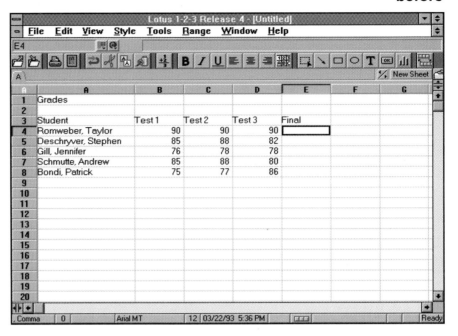

Oops!

To undo a calculation, immediately choose the Edit Undo command.

1. **Click on cell E4.**

   E4 is the cell that will contain the formula to calculate an average.

2. **Type @AVG(.**

   @AVG is the name of the function that automatically averages entries in a range. You enter the range within the parentheses. (You can type the function in either uppercase or lowercase letters.)

3. **Select the range B4..D4.**

   This step selects the range that you want to average. In the contents box, you see @AVG(B4..D4.

   For help with this step, see *TASK: Select a range.*

4. **Press Enter.**

   Pressing Enter confirms the formula and adds the closing parenthesis. You see the results of the function in the cell. If you want, you can finish the worksheet by copying E4 to the range E5..E8.

after

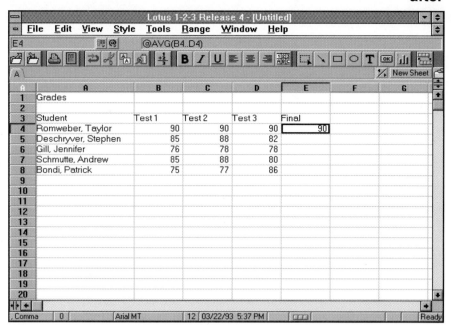

If you hear a beep and the entry won't enter into the cell, you've made a mistake. Check your typing carefully. If you want, press the Esc key and start over.

REVIEW

1. Click on the cell where you want the average to appear.

2. Type **@AVG(**.

3. Select the range that you want to average.

4. Press **Enter**.

To calculate an average

Try some other functions

1-2-3 offers many functions that can help you figure anything from loan payments to investment returns. See *Using 1-2-3 Release 4.0 for Windows,* Special Edition, for more information.

Count items in a list

before

```
Lotus 1-2-3 Release 4 - [Untitled]
File  Edit  View  Style  Tools  Range  Window  Help
B10                    @
```

	A	B	C	D	E	F	G
1	Project Tracking						
2							
3	TASK	COMPLETE					
4	Drywall	16-Jul					
5	Electrical	18-Jul					
6	Plumbing	14-Aug					
7	Carpentry						
8	Painting						
9							
10	Tasks Complete						

```
Automatic        Arial MT      12 03/22/93 6:03 PM              Ready
```

Oops!

To undo the count, immediately choose the Edit Undo command.

1. Click on cell B10.

B10 is the cell that will contain the function.

2. Type @COUNT(.

@COUNT is the name of the function that counts the number of entries in a range. You enter the range that you want to count within the parentheses. (You can type the function in either uppercase or lowercase letters.)

3. Select the range B4..B8.

This step selects the range that you want to count. In the contents box, you see @COUNT(B4..B8.

For help with this step, see *TASK: Select a range*.

4. Press Enter.

Pressing Enter confirms the formula and adds the closing parenthesis. You see the results of the function in cell B10.

after

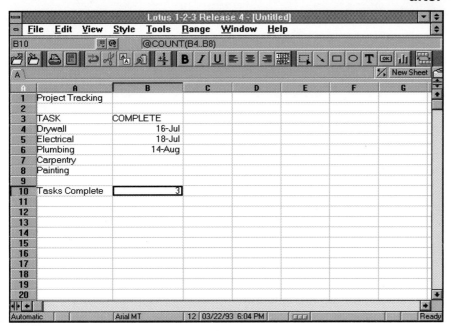

What's that beep?

If you hear a beep and the entry won't enter into the cell, you've made a mistake. Check your typing carefully. If you want, press the Esc key and start over.

REVIEW

1. Click on the cell where you want the count to appear.

2. Type **@COUNT(**.

3. Select the range that you want to count.

4. Press **Enter**.

To count items in a list

Figure out a loan payment

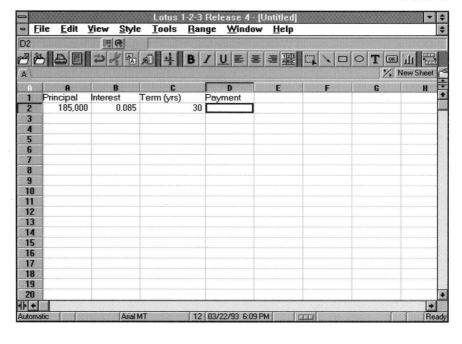

1. **Enter the values shown in the Before screen.**

   This step enters the principal, interest, and term.

2. **Click on cell D2.**

   D2 is the cell that will contain the function.

3. **Type @PMT(A2;B2/12;C2*12).**

   @PMT is the name of the function that automatically figures a loan payment. The entries in parentheses are the *arguments* for the function. Don't type any spaces, and type a semicolon between each argument.

   The second two arguments (interest and term) have to be converted to like items (months). You do this by multiplying the term by 12 and by dividing the interest rate by 12.

4. **Press Enter.**

   Pressing Enter confirms the function and tells you the monthly payment for this loan.

after

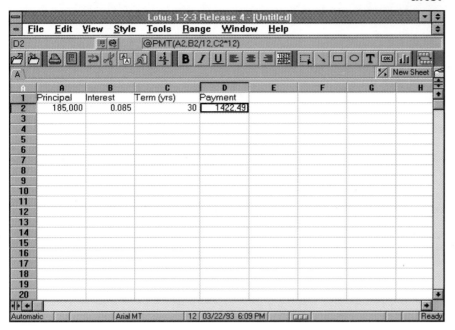

Use other functions

1-2-3 offers many functions that can help you figure anything from averages to investment returns. See *Using 1-2-3 Release 4.0 for Windows,* Special Edition, for more information.

REVIEW

1. Click on the cell where you want the function to appear.

2. Type **@PMT**(*principal;interest;term*). For *principal*, *interest*, and *term*, type the values or point to cells that contain the values.

3. Press **Enter**.

To figure out a loan payment

More Formatting

This section includes the following tasks:

Boldface cell contents

Italicize cell contents

Underline cell contents

Change the font

Change the font size

Change the color

Add a border to cells

Outline cells

Shade cells

Show negative numbers in red

Change the orientation of cells

Draw an arrow

Boldface cell contents

Bold SmartIcon

before

```
─  ▼                    Lotus 1-2-3 Release 4 - [Untitled]                    ▼ ≑
─  File   Edit   View   Style   Tools   Range   Window   Help                    ≑
A3                      ≋@          'Last Name
[toolbar icons]  B  I  U  ≡ ≡ ≡ ▦   ▭ ╲ ▭ ○ T ◰ ▥ ▦
A ╲                                                        ⅍ New Sheet
```

	A	B	C	D	E	F	G
1	Client List						
2							
3	Last Name	First Name	Phone	Price			
4	Ball	Raymond	555-2278	500000			
5	Dulin	Bret	555-1644	125000			
6	Gerdt	Sunnya	555-8711	90000			
7	Moore	Steve	555-9000	250000			
8							
9							
10							
11							
12							
13							
14							
15							
16							
17							
18							
19							
20							

```
Automatic        Arial MT        12  03/22/93  6:28 PM        ▭▭▭        Ready
```

Oops!

Choose the Edit Undo command immediately to reverse the change. Or click on the Bold SmartIcon again to turn off bold.

1. **Select the range A3..D3.**

   This step selects the range that you want to make bold. See *TASK: Select a range* for help with this step.

2. **Click on the Bold SmartIcon.**

   This step makes the range bold. The range is still selected. Click on any cell to deselect the range.

after

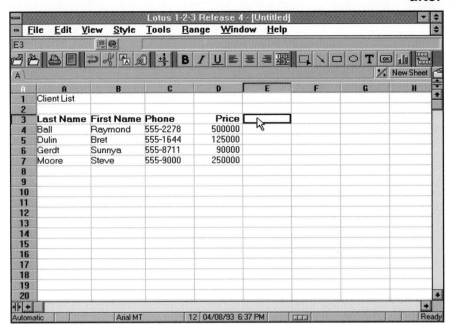

Use a different method

You also can turn on bold by opening the Font & Attributes dialog box from the Style menu and clicking on the Bold option in the Attributes area. See *TASK: Change the font* to learn how to open the Font & Attributes dialog box.

REVIEW

1. Select the cell or range you want to make bold.

2. Click on the **Bold** SmartIcon.

To boldface cell contents

Italicize cell contents

Italic SmartIcon

```
┌─────────────────────────────────────────────────────────────┐
│ ─                 Lotus 1-2-3 Release 4 - [Untitled]      ▼ ▲ │
│ ─  File   Edit   View   Style   Tools   Range   Window   Help │
│ A3              ▦ @         'Item                             │
│ [icons]  B I U ...                          New Sheet        │
│ A                                                            │
│      A          B       C        D       E    F    G    H    │
│  1  Sales Plan                                               │
│  2                                                           │
│  3  Item       Cost    Price           Profit               │
│  4  T-shirts      8      30       22                         │
│  5  Dolls         5      25       20                         │
│  6  Beaded shoes  8      40       32                         │
│  7  Quilt        10      45       35                         │
│  8  Wreaths       6      30       24                         │
│  9                                                           │
│ 10                                                           │
│ 11                                                           │
│ 12                                                           │
│ 13                                                           │
│ 14                                                           │
│ 15                                                           │
│ 16                                                           │
│ 17                                                           │
│ 18                                                           │
│ 19                                                           │
│ 20                                                           │
│ Automatic        Arial MT        12  03/22/93 6:31 PM  Ready │
└─────────────────────────────────────────────────────────────┘
```

Oops!

Choose the Edit Undo command immediately to reverse the change. Or click on the Italic SmartIcon again to turn off italic.

1. **Select the range A3..D3.**

   This step selects the range that you want to italicize. See *TASK: Select a range* for help with this step.

2. **Click on the Italic SmartIcon.**

   The cell contents appear in italic. The range is still selected. Click on any cell to deselect the range.

after

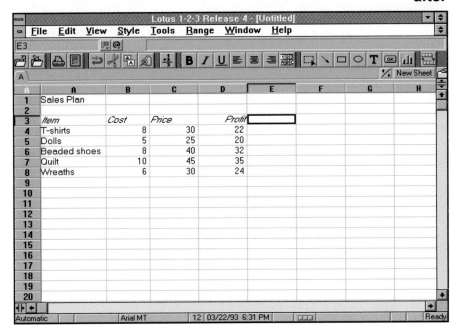

Use a different method

You also can make a cell's contents italic by opening the Font & Attributes dialog box from the Style menu and clicking on the Italic option in the Attributes area. See *TASK: Change the font* to learn how to open the Font & Attributes dialog box.

REVIEW

1. Select the cell or range you want to italicize.

2. Click on the Italic SmartIcon.

To italicize cell contents

More Formatting

Underline cell contents

Underline SmartIcon

before

Lotus 1-2-3 Release 4 - [CHKREG.WK4]

File   Edit   View   Style   Tools   Range   Window   Help

A3   "Number

B *I* U

A

	A	B	C	D	E	F	G	H
1	Check Register							
2								
3	Number	Date	Payee	Amount				
4	100	07/13	Altas	$75.99				
5	101	07/15	The Gap	$45.88				
6	102	07/16	Cash	$25.00				
7	103	07/18	Sams	$100.23				
8	104	07/18	House	$1,250.00				
9	105	07/29	Shell	$91.21				
10								
11								
12								
13								
14								
15								
16								
17								
18								
19								
20								

New Sheet

Automatic   Arial MT   12   03/22/93 6:35 PM   Ready

Oops!

Choose the Edit Undo command immediately to reverse the change. Or click on the Underline SmartIcon again to turn off underlining.

1. **Select the range A3..D3.**

   This step selects the range that you want to underline. See *TASK: Select a range* for help with this step.

2. **Click on the Underline SmartIcon.**

   The cell contents are underlined. The range is still selected. Click on any cell to deselect the range.

after

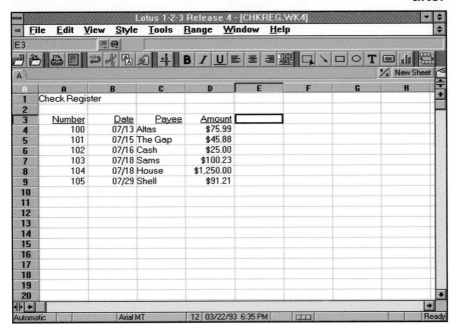

You also can underline by opening the Font & Attributes dialog box from the Style menu and clicking on the Underline option in the Attributes area. See *TASK: Change the font* to learn how to open the Font & Attributes dialog box.

REVIEW

1. Select the cell or range that you want to underline.

2. Click on the **Underline** SmartIcon.

To underline cell contents

Change the font

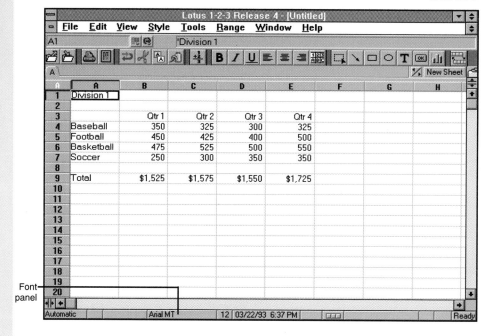

Font panel

1. **Click on cell A1.**

   A1 is the cell that you want to change.

2. **Click on Style in the menu bar.**

   This step opens the Style menu. You see a list of Style commands.

3. **Click on Font & Attributes.**

   This step chooses the Font & Attributes command. You see the Font & Attributes dialog box with a list of the fonts your printer can use.

4. **Click on Times.**

   This step selects the Times font. If you don't have this font, select one that you do have.

5. **Click on OK.**

   This step confirms the new font. You see the font change on-screen. The status bar displays the new font.

after

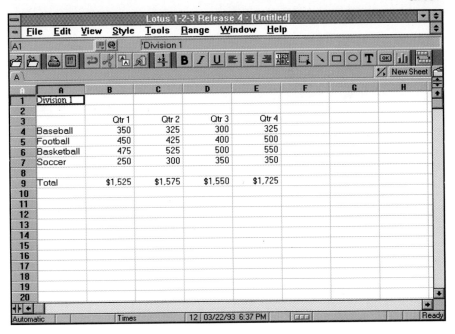

Use other options

You can also specify style (bold, italic, and so on) from the Fonts & Attributes dialog box. Click on the option you want in the Attribute area. For complete information on all options, see *Using 1-2-3 Release 4.0 for Windows*, Special Edition.

REVIEW

To change the font

1. Select the cell or range you want to change.

2. Click on **Style** in the menu bar.

3. Click on the **Font & Attributes** command.

4. Click on the font you want in the Fonts list.

5. Click on **OK**.

Try a shortcut

Click on the Font panel in the status bar to display a list of fonts. Then select the font you want.

More Formatting

Change the font size

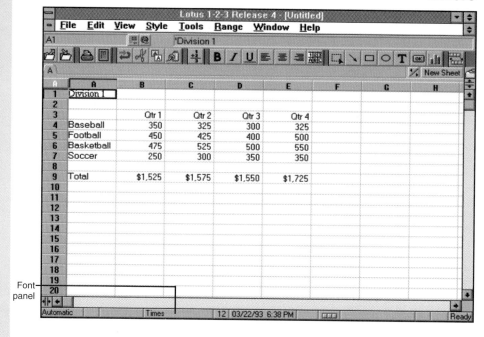

Font panel

Oops!

To undo the font change, immediately choose the Edit Undo command.

1. **Click on cell A1.**

   A1 is the cell that you want to change.

2. **Click on Style in the menu bar.**

   This step opens the Style menu. You see a list of Style commands.

3. **Click on Font & Attributes.**

   This step selects the Font & Attributes command. The Font & Attributes dialog box appears and lists the current fonts.

4. **Click on 24 in the Size list.**

   This step selects 24-point size. If you don't have this font size, select one that you do have.

5. **Click on OK.**

   You see the font change on-screen. The status bar displays the new format.

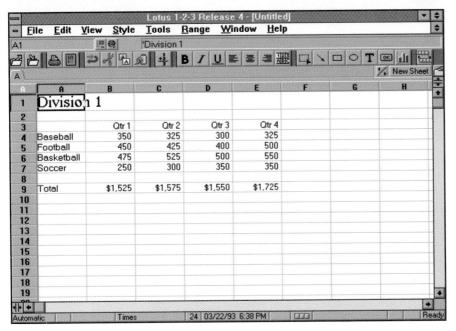

You can also specify style (bold, italic, and so on) from the Fonts & Attributes dialog box. Click on the option you want in the Attribute area. For complete information on all options, see *Using 1-2-3 Release 4.0 for Windows*, Special Edition.

REVIEW

1. Select the cell or range you want to change.

2. Click on **Style** in the menu bar.

3. Click on the **Font & Attributes** command.

4. Click on the font size in the Size list.

5. Click on **OK**.

To change the font size

Click on the Font Size panel in the status bar to display a list of fonts. Then select the font size you want.

More Formatting

Change the color

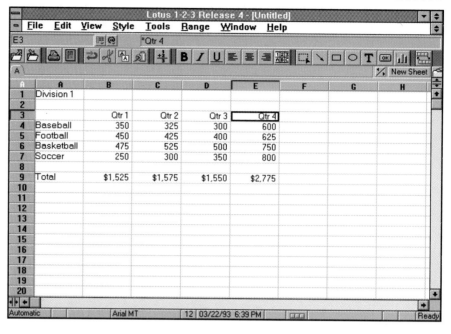

To undo the color change, immediately choose the Edit Undo command.

1. **Select the range E3..E9.**

   This step selects the range you want to change. See *TASK: Select a range* for help with this step.

2. **Click on Style in the menu bar.**

   This step opens the Style menu. You see a list of Style commands.

3. **Click on Font & Attributes.**

   This step chooses the Font & Attributes command. You see the Font & Attributes dialog box.

4. **Click on the down arrow next to Color.**

   This step displays a palette of colors.

5. **Click on any shade of blue in the color palette.**

   This step selects the color blue.

6. **Click on OK.**

   This step verifies the color change. You see the color change on-screen.

   The range is still selected. Click on any cell to deselect the range.

after

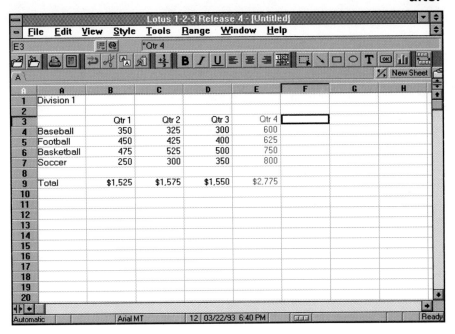

**Make negative
numbers red**

To have 1-2-3 display all
negative numbers in
red, see *TASK: Show
negative numbers in
red.*

REVIEW

To change the color

1. Select the cell or range you want to change.

2. Click on **Style** in the menu bar.

3. Click on the **Font & Attributes** command.

4. Click on the down arrow next to Color.

5. Click on the color in the color palette.

6. Click on **OK**.

Use other options

You can also specify
style (bold, italic, and so
on) from the Fonts &
Attributes dialog box.
Click on the option you
want in the Attribute
area. For complete
information on all
options, see *Using
1-2-3 Release 4.0 for
Windows*, Special
Edition.

Add a border to cells

before

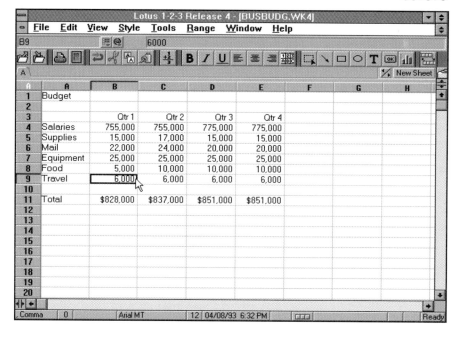

1. **Select the range B9..E9.**

   This step selects the range that you want to add a border to. See *TASK: Select a range* for help with this step.

2. **Click on Style in the menu bar.**

   This step opens the Style menu. You see a list of Style commands.

3. **Click on Lines & Color.**

   This step selects the Lines & Color command. You see the Lines & Color dialog box. In the Border area of this box, you can select which side of the cell to add a line to. You can select the line style among other available selections.

4. **Click in the Bottom check box.**

   This step tells 1-2-3 to add a border to the bottom of the cells. The check box should have an X in it.

5. **Click on OK.**

   This step verifies adding the border. Because you didn't specify a line style, 1-2-3 uses the default line style: a thin line. On-screen, the range is underlined. (The line may be hard to see with the worksheet gridlines.)

   The range is still selected. Click on any cell to deselect the range.

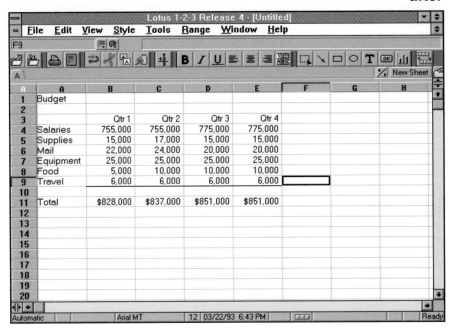

Other line options

See *Using 1-2-3 Release 4.0 for Windows,* Special Edition, to learn more about the available line styles and options.

R E V I E W

1. Select the cell or range you want to add a border to.

2. Click on **Style** in the menu bar.

3. Click on the **Lines & Color** command.

4. Click in the check boxes of the side(s) you want to add a border to.

5. From the drop-down list, click on the line style you want.

6. Click on **OK**.

To add a border to cells

Outline cells

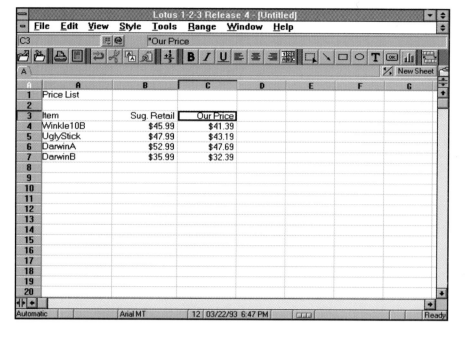

1. **Select the range C3..C7.**

   This step selects the range that you want to outline. See *TASK: Select a range* for help with this step.

2. **Click on Style in the menu bar.**

   This step opens the Style menu. You see a list of Style commands.

3. **Click on Lines & Color.**

   This step selects the Lines & Color command. You see the Lines & Color dialog box. In the Border area, you can select what to add a border to.

4. **Click in the Outline check box.**

   This step selects the Outline check box. An X appears in the check box so that you know that this option is selected.

5. **Click on OK.**

   This step confirms outlining the range. On-screen the range is outlined. The outline still may be hard to see because of the gridlines on the screen display.

   The range is still selected. Click on any cell to deselect the range.

after

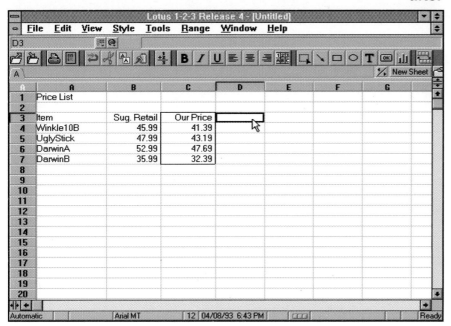

Other line options

See *Using 1-2-3 Release 4.0 for Windows,* Special Edition, to learn more about the available line styles and options.

REVIEW

1. Select the cell or range you want to outline.

2. Click on **Style** in the menu bar.

3. Click on the **Lines & Color** command.

4. Click in the **Outline** check box.

5. Click on **OK**.

To outline cells

Shade cells

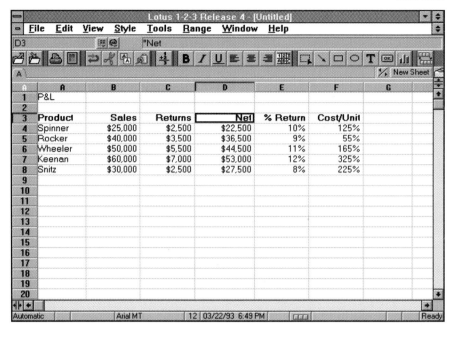

1. **Select the range D3..D8.**

   This step selects the range that you want to shade. See *TASK: Select a range* for help with this step.

2. **Click on Style in the menu bar.**

   This step opens the Style menu. You see a list of Style commands.

3. **Click on Lines & Color.**

   This step selects the Lines & Color command. You see the Lines & Color dialog box.

4. **Click on the down arrow next to Patterns.**

   This step displays a palette of patterns.

5. **Click on the second-to-last pattern in the top row.**

   This step selects the new pattern.

6. **Click on OK.**

   This step confirms the change. You see the pattern on-screen.

   The range is still selected. Click outside the range to deselect it.

after

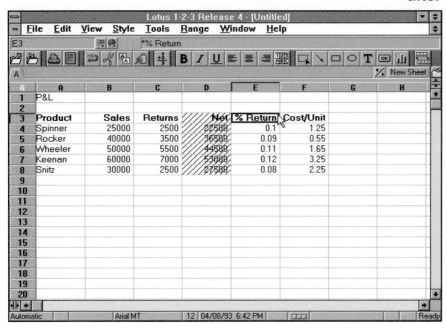

Want to know more?

You can also select other patterns, a background pattern, and a text color in the Interior area of the Lines & Color dialog box. Refer to *Using 1-2-3 Release 4.0 for Windows*, Special Edition, to learn more.

REVIEW

1. Select the cell or range to shade.

2. Click on **Style** in the menu bar.

3. Click on the **Lines & Colors** command.

4. Click on the down arrow next to Patterns.

5. Click on the pattern you want.

6. Click on **OK**.

To shade cells

Show negative numbers in red

Click here

```
┌─────────────────────────────────────────────────────────────────────┐
│                  Lotus 1-2-3 Release 4 - [Untitled]            ▼  ▲   │
│ ─  File   Edit   View   Style   Tools   Range   Window   Help     ▲  │
│ A1                    ▦ @      'Statement                            │
│ [toolbar icons]  B  I  U  ≡ ≡ ≡                    ▼   New Sheet     │
│  A │     A       │    B    │    C    │    D    │    E    │  F  │  G  │
│  1 │ Statement   │         │         │         │         │     │     │
│  2 │             │         │         │         │         │     │     │
│  3 │ Venture     │  Sales  │ Returns │  Cost   │   Net   │     │     │
│  4 │ Spinner     │ $25,000 │ $15,000 │ $15,000 │($5,000) │     │     │
│  5 │ Rocker      │ $40,000 │  $3,500 │  $3,500 │ $33,000 │     │     │
│  6 │ Wheeler     │ $50,000 │  $4,500 │  $6,000 │ $39,500 │     │     │
│  7 │ Keenan      │ $60,000 │  $2,700 │  $8,000 │ $49,300 │     │     │
│  8 │ Snitz       │ $30,000 │  $7,000 │ $13,000 │ $10,000 │     │     │
│  9 │ Gooch       │ $12,000 │  $9,000 │  $5,000 │($2,000) │     │     │
│ 10 │             │         │         │         │         │     │     │
│ 11 │             │         │         │         │         │     │     │
│ 12 │             │         │         │         │         │     │     │
│ 13 │             │         │         │         │         │     │     │
│ 14 │             │         │         │         │         │     │     │
│ 15 │             │         │         │         │         │     │     │
│ 16 │             │         │         │         │         │     │     │
│ 17 │             │         │         │         │         │     │     │
│ 18 │             │         │         │         │         │     │     │
│ 19 │             │         │         │         │         │     │     │
│ 20 │             │         │         │         │         │     │     │
│ Automatic        │ Arial MT      │ 12 │03/22/93 6:56 PM│      │Ready │
└─────────────────────────────────────────────────────────────────────┘
```

Oops!

To turn off this option, follow these same steps. Make sure that the Negative values in red check box doesn't contain an X.

1. **Click on the A to the left of the column letters and above the row numbers.**

   This step selects the entire worksheet.

2. **Click on Style in the menu bar.**

   This step opens the Style menu. You see a list of Style commands.

3. **Click on Lines & Color.**

   This step selects the Lines & Color command. You see the Lines & Color dialog box.

4. **Click in the Negative values in red check box.**

   This step turns on this option. An X appears in the check box.

5. **Click on OK.**

   This step confirms the change. All negative numbers are now displayed in red.

   The range is still selected. Click on any cell to deselect the range.

after

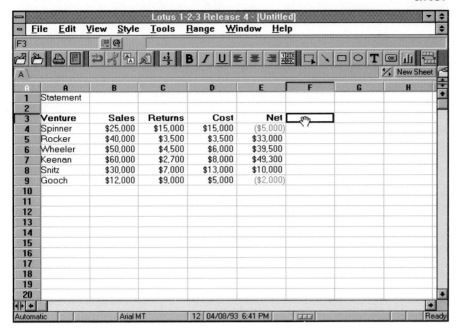

1. Click on the worksheet tab to select the entire worksheet.

2. Click on **Style** in the menu bar.

3. Click on the **Lines & Colors** command.

4. Click in the **Negative values in red** check box.

5. Click on **OK**.

To show negative numbers in red

More Formatting

Change the orientation of cells

```
═    Lotus 1-2-3 Release 4 - [Untitled]            ▼ ◆
□  File  Edit  View  Style  Tools  Range  Window  Help        ◆
A3            ▦◎      'SO1
```

	A	B	C	D	E	F	G	H
1								
2								
3	SO1	125,000						
4	SO2	235,000						
5	SO3	450,000						
6	SO4	125,000						
7								
8								
9								
10								
11								
12								
13								
14								
15								
16								
17								
18								
19								
20								

```
Automatic        Arial MT        12 03/22/93 6:59 PM   ▭▭▭      Ready
```

Oops!

To undo the change, select the Edit Undo command.

1. **Select the range A3..A6.**

   This step selects the range that you want to change. For help with this step, see *TASK: Select a range*.

2. **Click on Style in the menu bar.**

   This step opens the Style menu. You see a list of Style commands.

3. **Click on Alignment.**

   This step selects the Alignment command and displays the Alignment dialog box.

4. **Click on down arrow next to the Orientation box.**

   This step displays the two orientations you can choose.

5. **Click on the abc option that goes vertically down the cells.**

   This step selects the orientation you want.

6. **Click on OK.**

   This step confirms the command, and the range is formatted. The range is still selected. Click on any cell to deselect the range.

Easy 1-2-3 for Windows

after

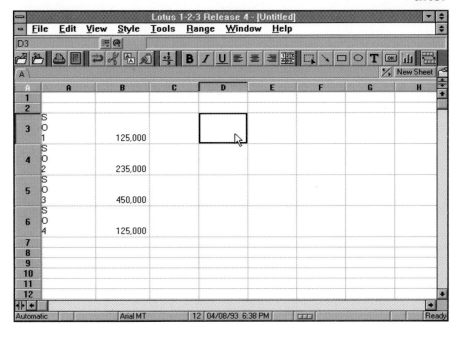

REVIEW

1. Select the cell or range you want to change.

2. Click on **Style** in the menu bar.

3. Click on the **Alignment** command.

4. Click on the down arrow next to the Orientation box.

5. Click on the abc option you want.

6. Click on **OK**.

To change the orientation of cells

More Formatting

181

Draw an arrow

Arrow SmartIcon

```
Lotus 1-2-3 Release 4 - [Untitled]
File   Edit   View   Style   Tools   Range   Window   Help
G7                    @
A                                                          New Sheet
```

	A	B	C	D	E	F	G	H
1	Division 2							
2								
3		Qtr 1	Qtr 2	Qtr 3	Qtr 4			
4	Baseball	450	350	400	1000			
5	Football	450	425	400	650			
6	Basketball	775	525	500	825			
7	Soccer	250	500	450	750			
8								
9	Total	1925	1800	1750	3225			
10								
11								
12								
13								
14								
15								
16								
17								
18								
19								
20								

```
Automatic          Arial MT          12  04/08/93  6:49 PM               Ready
```

Oops!

To delete the arrow, immediately choose the Edit Undo command. Or click anywhere on the arrow to select it; then press the Del key.

1. **Click on the Arrow SmartIcon.**

   This step selects the Arrow SmartIcon.

2. **Point the mouse pointer somewhere near cell G7 and hold down the mouse button.**

   This step tells 1-2-3 where to start the arrow.

3. **Drag to cell E9.**

   This step draws the arrow on-screen that points to cell E9. You can add other objects—circles, squares, text.

4. **Release the mouse button.**

   The arrow is selected. Notice that when the arrow is selected, the SmartIcons change and additional drawing icons appear.

after

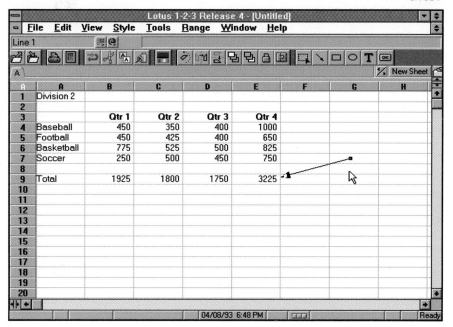

Want to know more?

1-2-3 offers several drawing tools to spiff up your spreadsheets. If you want to know more about them, see *Using 1-2-3 Release 4.0 for Windows,* Special Edition.

REVIEW

1. Click on the **Arrow** SmartIcon.

2. Click where you want the start of the arrow.

3. Drag to draw the arrow.

4. Release the mouse button.

To draw an arrow

Printing

This section includes the following tasks:

Preview a worksheet

Add a header

Add a footer

Set margins

Change the print orientation

Print a worksheet

Preview a worksheet

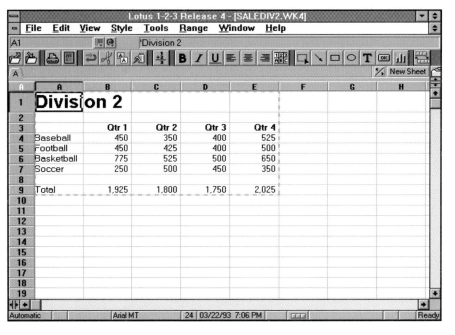

Oops!

When you are finished looking at the preview, click on the preview page or press the Esc key.

1. **Click on File in the menu bar.**

   This step opens the File menu. You see a list of File commands.

2. **Click on Print Preview.**

   This step chooses the Print Preview command. You see the Print Preview dialog box. The default, Current worksheet, is selected.

3. **Click on OK.**

   This step tells 1-2-3 that you want to view the current worksheet. You see an on-screen preview of how your worksheet will look when printed.

   Note that the Before and After screens show a worksheet with some formatting changes.

after

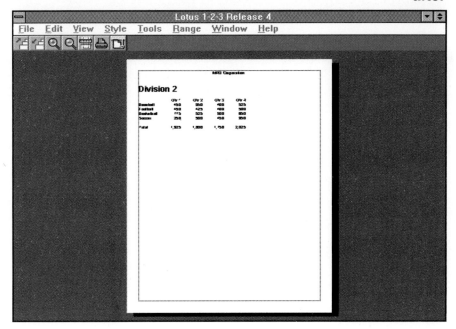

1. Click on **File** in the menu bar.

2. Click on the **Print Preview** command.

3. Click on **OK**.

4. Click the mouse button or press **Esc** to exit the preview.

To preview a worksheet

Printing

187

Add a header

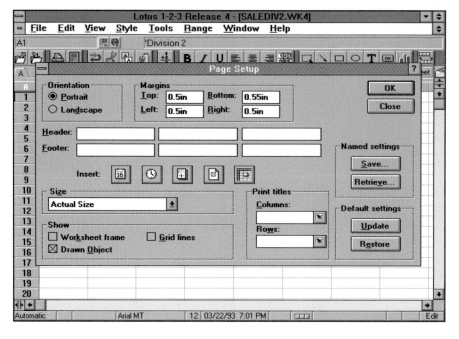

1. Click on **File** in the menu bar.

   This step opens the File menu. You see a list of File commands.

2. Click on **Page Setup**.

   This step chooses the Page Setup command. You see the Page Setup dialog box. The Before screen shows this step.

3. Click in the center **Header** text box.

   You can insert headers in three different areas of the top part of the page: left, center, and right. This step selects the center position. The Before screen shows this step.

4. Type **MRO Corporation**.

   This step enters the header text.

5. Click on **OK**.

   This step verifies that you want to add the header. On-screen, you cannot see the header. To do so, you must preview the worksheet (see *TASK: Preview a worksheet*). The After screen shows a preview of the worksheet.

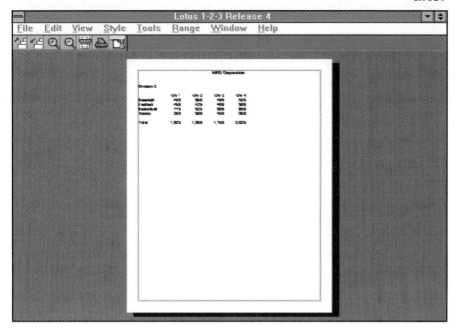

1. Click on **File** in the menu bar.

2. Click on the **Page Setup** command.

3. Click in the appropriate **Header** text box.

4. Type the text for the header.

5. Click on **OK**.

To add a header

Add a footer

Page number icon

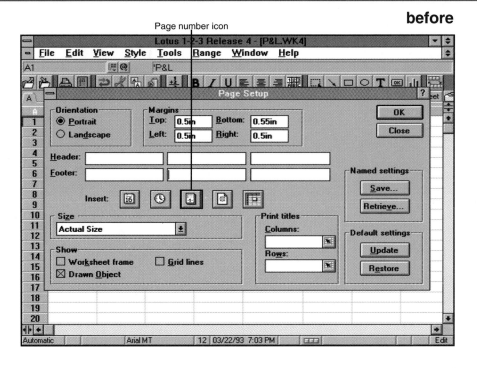

1. Click on **File** in the menu bar.

   This step opens the File menu. You see a list of File commands.

2. Click on **Page Setup**.

   This step chooses the Page Setup command. You see the Page Setup dialog box. This dialog box specifies how the worksheet is printed.

3. Click in the center **Footer** text box.

   You can insert footers in three different areas of the bottom part of the page: left, center, and right. This step selects the center position. The Before screen shows this step.

4. Click on the **Page Number** icon next to the Insert options.

   This step inserts a code (#) that tells 1-2-3 to insert the page number. When you print the document, the code will be replaced by the appropriate page number.

5. Click on **OK**.

   This step verifies that you want to add the footer. On-screen, you cannot see the footer. To do so, you must preview the worksheet. (see *TASK: Preview a worksheet*). The After screen shows a preview of the worksheet.

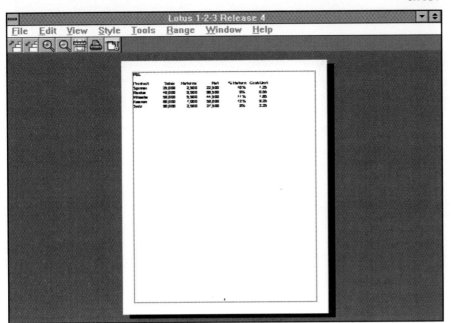

Want to know more?

For more information on headers and footers, see *Using 1-2-3 Release 4.0 for Windows,* Special Edition.

REVIEW

1. Click on **File** in the menu bar.

2. Click on the **Page Setup** command.

3. Click in the appropriate **Footer** text box.

4. Type the text for the footer or click the icon of the item you want in the footer (such as page number).

5. Click on **OK**.

To add a footer

Set margins

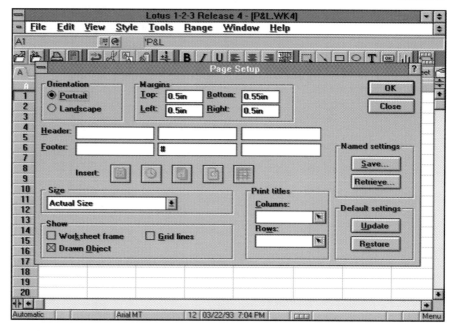

Choose the Edit Undo command immediately to undo the change—even before you preview the document. Or follow this same procedure to reset margins to the default.

1. Click on **File** in the menu bar.

   This step opens the File menu. You see a list of File commands.

2. Click on **Page Setup**.

   This step chooses the Page Setup command. You see the Page Setup dialog box, which displays information about the current page setup. (For complete information on all the options in this box, see *Using 1-2-3 Release 4.0 for Windows,* Special Edition.)

   The Before screen shows this step.

3. Click in the **Top** text box in the Margins area.

   This step selects the Top margin setting—the setting that you want to change.

4. Delete the current entry.

   Use the Backspace or Del key to delete the current entry.

5. Type **2**.

   This step sets the new top margin to two inches. 1-2-3 will automatically insert the *in* after *2*.

after

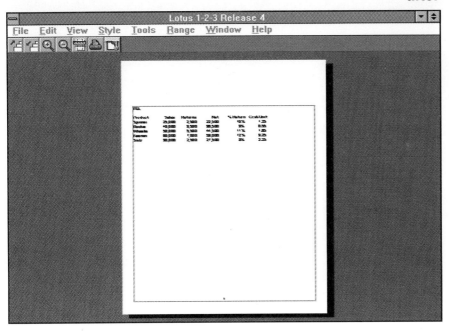

6. Click on **OK**.

This step verifies the margin change. You cannot see the new margins on-screen. To do so, you must preview the worksheet (see *TASK: Preview a worksheet*). The After screen shows a preview of the worksheet.

1. Click on **File** in the menu bar.

2. Click on the **Page Setup** command.

3. Click in the appropriate text box (**Top**, **Bottom**, **Left**, or **Right**) of the Margin area.

4. Delete the current entry.

5. Type the new margin.

6. Click on **OK**.

To set margins

Change the print orientation

before

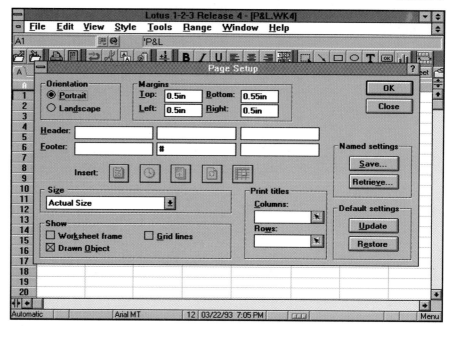

Oops!

To undo this change, choose the Edit Undo command immediately— even before you preview the document. Or follow this same procedure and select Portrait.

1. **Click on File in the menu bar.**

   This step opens the File menu. You see a list of File commands.

2. **Click on Page Setup.**

   This step chooses the Page Setup command. You see the Page Setup dialog box, which displays information about the current page setup. (For complete information on all the options in the Page Setup dialog box, see *Using 1-2-3 Release 4.0 for Windows*, Special Edition.)

   The Before screen shows this step.

3. **Click on Landscape in the Orientation area.**

   This step selects the Landscape option button and specifies landscape orientation. The circle next to Landscape is darkened.

4. **Click on OK.**

   This step verifies the change. You cannot see the new orientation on-screen. To do so, you must preview the worksheet. (see *TASK: Preview a worksheet*). The After screen shows a preview of the worksheet.

after

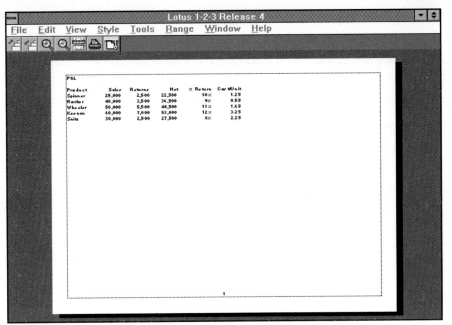

What's the difference?

In portrait orientation, the longest sides of the page run vertically. In landscape orientation, the longest sides of the page run horizontally.

REVIEW

1. Click on **File** in the menu bar.

2. Click on the **Page Setup** command.

3. Click on the option button of the orientation you want.

4. Click on **OK**.

To change the print orientation

Print a worksheet

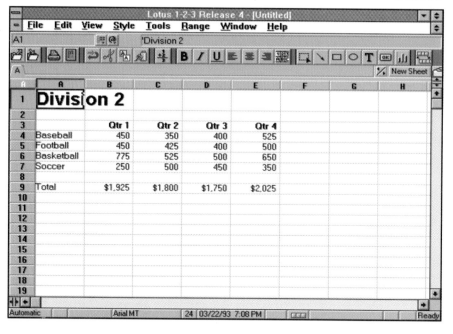

1. Click on **File** in the menu bar.

   This step opens the File menu. You see a list of File commands.

2. Click on **Print**.

   This step chooses the Print command, and the Print dialog box appears on-screen. The After screen shows this step.

3. Click on **OK**.

   This step starts the print job. On-screen the worksheet area that contains data is bordered with a gray fence. This fence indicates the *print range*—the area of the worksheet that will be printed.

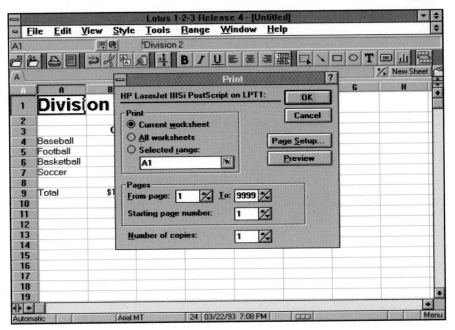

1-2-3 has lots of print options and features. For complete information about printing—printing only certain pages, printing multiple copies, and so on—see *Using 1-2-3 Release 4.0 for Windows*, Special Edition.

REVIEW

1. Click on **File** in the menu bar.

2. Click on the **Print** command.

3. Click on **OK**.

To print a worksheet

Try a shortcut

Press the Ctrl+P key combination to select the Print command. Or use the Print SmartIcon.

Creating Charts

This section includes the following tasks:

Create a chart

Move a chart

Resize a chart

Change a title

Delete a label

Change a label

Change the chart type

Save a chart

Rename a chart

Print a chart

Delete a chart

Create a chart

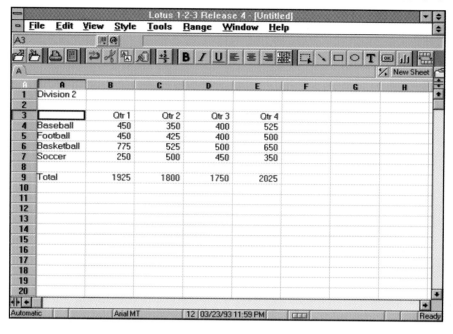

Oops!

To delete a chart that you've created, see *TASK: Delete a chart*.

1. **Select the range A3..E7.**

   This step selects the data that you want to chart. For help selecting a range, see *TASK: Select a range*. Don't include the totals in the range.

2. **Click on Tools in the menu bar.**

   This step opens the Tools menu. You see a list of Tools commands.

3. **Click on Chart.**

   This step chooses the Chart command. The mouse pointer changes shape when in the worksheet area.

4. **Click on cell A11.**

   This step tells 1-2-3 where to place the chart. A chart is created on the worksheet in the default type (2D bar) and size. You may not be able to see the entire chart. To see it all, scroll the worksheet.

   The chart is selected—handles appear around the edges, and the SmartIcons change to display icons for charts. You can change the chart size, location, and type when the chart is selected. See the other tasks in this section.

   Click outside of the chart to deselect it.

after

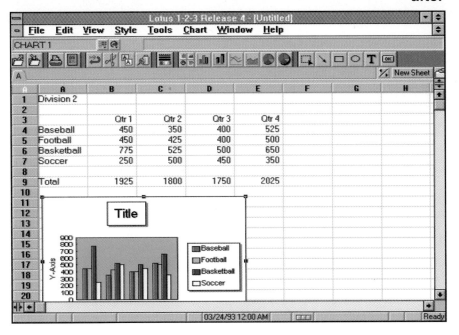

Want to know more?

1-2-3 has many different chart types, and you can customize the chart in numerous ways. For complete information on charts, see *Using 1-2-3 Release 4.0 for Windows,* Special Edition.

REVIEW

1. Select the range that you want to chart.

2. Click on **Tools** in the menu bar.

3. Click on the **Chart** command.

4. Click where you want to place the chart.

To create a chart

Try a shortcut

To create a chart quickly, select the range, and then click on the Chart SmartIcon.

Move a chart

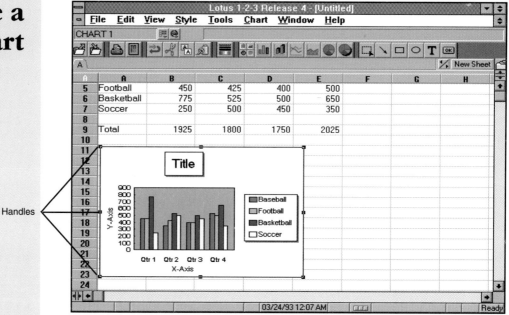

Handles

Follow this same procedure to return the chart to its original position.

1. **Click in one of the white areas of the chart and hold down the mouse button.**

   This step selects the chart. Be careful not to select individual items in the chart—the whole chart should be selected. Handles apepar on the outside of the entire chart when the entire chart is selected, and CHART1 appears in the selection indicator box.

2. **Drag the chart to the right.**

   This step moves the chart.

3. **Release the mouse button.**

   This step completes the move.

after

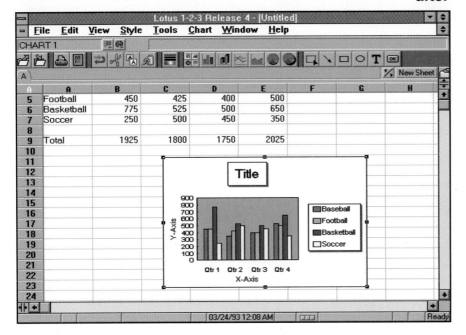

1. Click one of the white areas of the chart and hold down the mouse button.

2. Drag the chart to its new location.

3. Release the mouse button.

To move a chart

Resize a chart

before

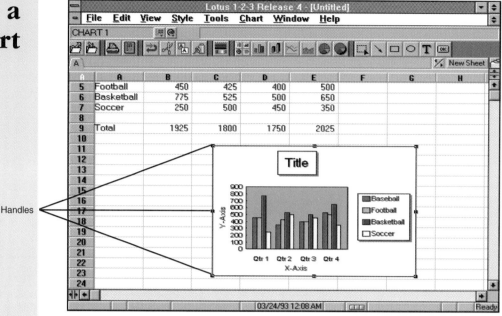

Handles

1. **Click on the chart.**

   This step selects the chart. Handles appear along the edges of the chart, and CHART1 appears in the selection indicator box.

2. **Click on the left border of the chart.**

   This step selects the side that you want to resize. The mouse pointer changes to a four-headed arrow.

3. **Click a handle, hold down the left mouse button, and drag to the left.**

   This step resizes the chart.

4. **Release the mouse button.**

   This step completes the change.

5. **Follow the same procedure to resize the chart from the bottom border.**

   This step resizes the lower side of the chart. You can click and drag any side of the chart. The After figure shows the worksheet scrolled somewhat.

after

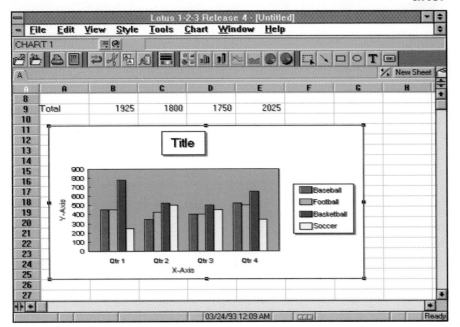

Move the chart

If the chart moves but isn't resized, you didn't click on a border. Try again.

REVIEW

1. Click on the chart to select it.

2. Drag the border that you want to resize.

To resize a chart

Change a title

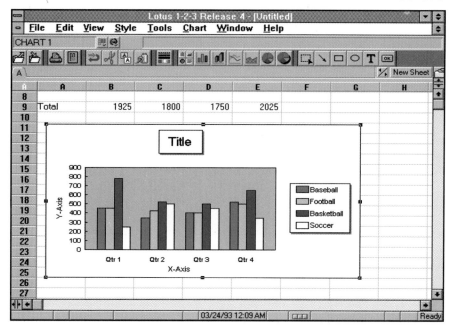

1. **Click on the chart.**

   This step selects the chart. Handles appear along the edges of the chart, and CHART1 appears in the selection indicator box.

2. **Click on Chart in the menu bar.**

   This step opens the Chart menu. You see a list of Chart commands.

3. **Click on Headings.**

   This step chooses the Headings command. The Headings dialog box appears, and the Title Line 1 text box is selected.

4. **Type Projected Sales.**

   This step enters the text for the title.

5. **Click on OK.**

   This step affirms the new title and closes the dialog box. You see the new title on-screen.

after

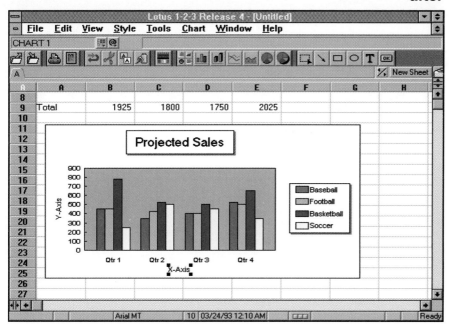

Try a shortcut

To change the title
quickly, double-click on
the title text box and
type the new title.

1. Select the chart.

2. Click on **Chart** in the menu bar.

3. Click on the **Headings** command.

4. Type the new title.

5. Click on **OK**.

To change a title

Want to know more?

1-2-3 has many different
chart types, and you
can customize the chart
in many ways. For com-
plete information on
charts, see *Using 1-2-3
Release 4.0 for
Windows,* Special
Edition.

Delete a label

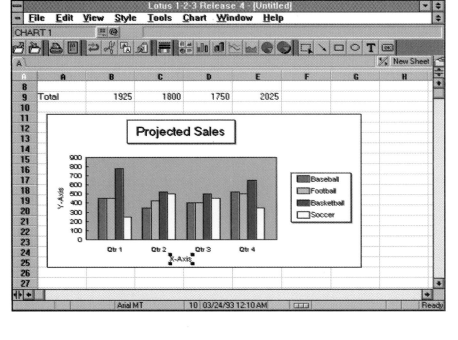

1. **Click on the X-Axis label.**

   This step selects the label. You see handles around the edges
   of the label. The X-Axis label is along the horizontal axis of
   the chart.

2. **Press Del.**

   Pressing the Del key deletes this label. The whole chart is now
   selected and the bottom border has moved up.

after

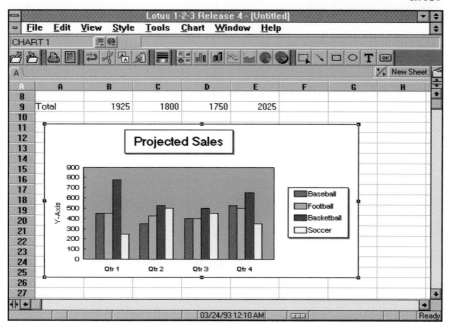

1-2-3 offers numerous ways that you can customize the labels and other chart elements. If you want to know more about these options, see *Using 1-2-3 Release 4.0 for Windows,* Special Edition.

REVIEW

1. Click on the label.

2. Press **Del**.

To delete a label

Change a label

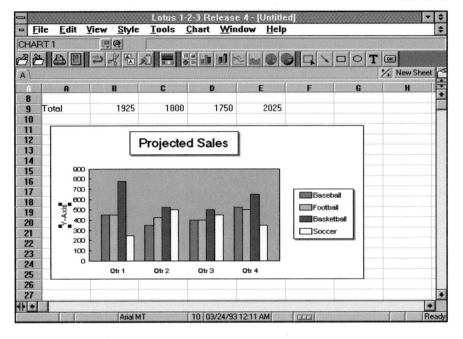

1. **Double-click on the Y-Axis label.**

   The y-axis label is along the vertical axis of the chart. This step selects the label and opens the Y-Axis dialog box. The insertion point is positioned in the Axis title text box.

2. **Type In thousands.**

   This step enters the new label.

3. **Click on OK.**

   This step confirms the change.

after

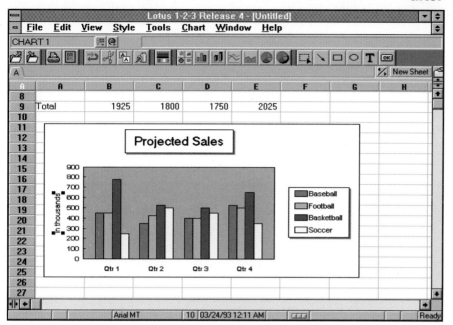

Use some other options

1-2-3 offers numerous ways that you can customize the labels and other chart elements. If you want to know more about these options, see *Using 1-2-3 Release 4.0 for Windows,* Special Edition.

REVIEW

1. Double-click on the label.

2. Type the new label.

3. Click on OK.

To change a label

Change the chart type

before

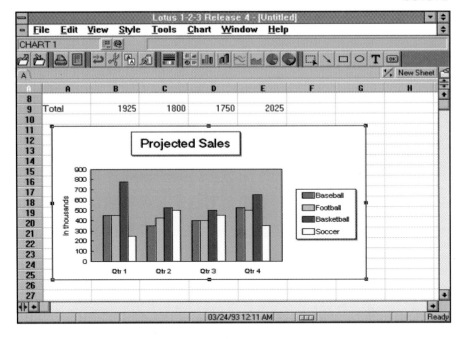

1. **Click on the chart.**

   This step selects the chart. Handles appear along the edges of the chart, and CHART1 appears in the selection indicator box.

2. **Click on Chart in the menu bar.**

   This step opens the Chart menu. You see a list of Chart commands.

3. **Click on Type.**

   This step chooses the Type command. The Type dialog box appears, and the types are listed along the left side of the dialog box. Chart styles appear in the middle of the dialog box.

4. **Click on the 3D Bar option button.**

   This step selects a new chart type.

5. **Click on OK.**

   This step confirms the change. The chart is changed to the new type and the Type dialog box disappears.

after

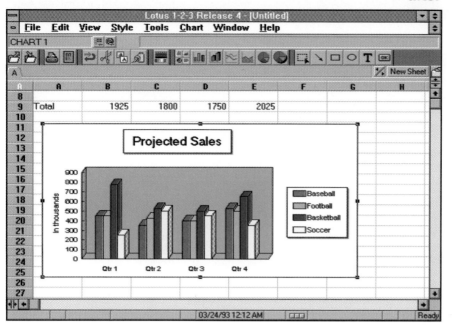

You also can select a different style for the chart. When you select the type, visual representations of the styles appear next to the type list. Click on the style you want.

1. Click on the chart to select it.

2. Click on **Chart** in the menu bar.

3. Click on the **Type** command.

4. In the Types section, click on the option button for the type of chart you want.

5. Click on the style you want.

6. Click on **OK**.

To change the chart type

Want to know more?

1-2-3 has many different chart types, and you can customize the chart in numerous ways. For complete information on charts, see *Using 1-2-3 Release 4.0 for Windows,* Special Edition.

Save a chart

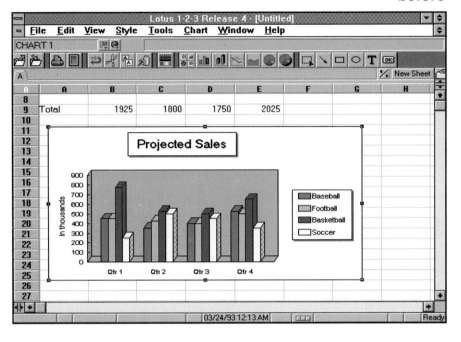

Oops!

If you change your mind and don't want to save the chart, click on Cancel for step 4.

1. **Click on File in the menu bar.**

   This step opens the File menu. You see a list of File commands.

2. **Click on Save.**

   This step chooses the Save command. Because this is the first time you are saving the file, the Save As dialog box appears.

3. **Type SALEPROJ.**

   This step assigns a name to the worksheet. 1-2-3 adds the WK4 extension.

4. **Click on OK.**

   You return to the worksheet. The chart is saved along with the worksheet. If you don't rename the chart, 1-2-3 assigns the name CHART*x*, where *x* is a sequential number—for instance, CHART1. When the chart is selected, this name appears in the selection indicator box. The new worksheet file title, SALEPROJ.WK4, appears in the title bar.

after

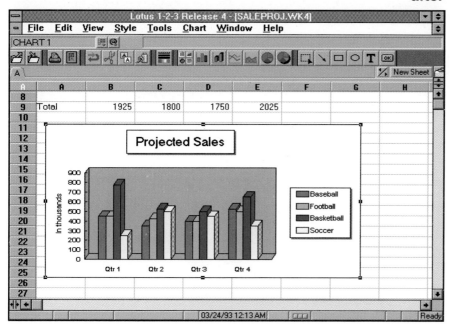

Rename the chart

If you don't like the default name, rename the chart. See *TASK: Rename a chart*.

REVIEW

1. Click on **File** in the menu bar.

2. Click on the **Save** command.

3. Type the file name, if you haven't already saved this file.

4. Click on **OK**.

To save a chart

Save the chart again

To save the worksheet file that contains a chart again, just choose the File Save command. You don't have to supply a file name.

TASK

Rename a chart

before

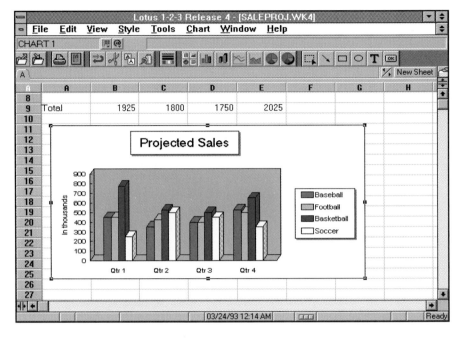

Oops!

Follow this same procedure to restore the original name.

1. **Click on the chart.**

   This step selects the chart. Handles appear along the edges of the chart.

2. **Click on Chart in the menu bar.**

   This step opens the Chart menu and displays a list of Chart commands.

3. **Click on Name.**

   This step chooses the Name command. You see the Chart Name dialog box.

4. **Type saleproj.**

   This step specifies the new name for the chart.

5. **Click on Rename.**

   This step confirms the name. When the chart is selected, this new name now appears in the selection indicator box.

after

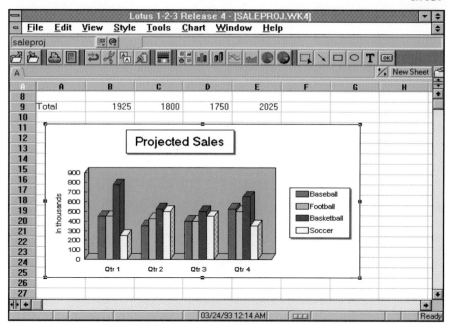

1. Click on the chart to select it.

2. Click on **Chart** in the menu bar.

3. Click on **Name**.

4. Type the name.

5. Click on **Rename**.

To rename a chart

Print a chart

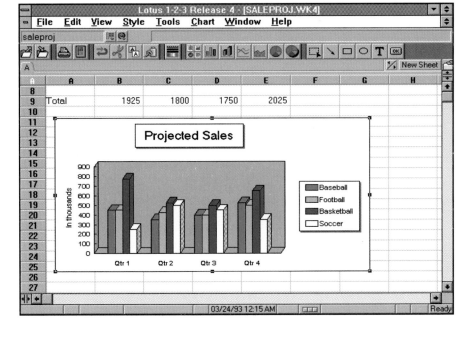

1. **Click on the chart.**

   This step selects the chart. Handles appear along the edges of the chart.

2. **Click on File in the menu bar.**

   This step opens the File menu. You see a list of File commands.

3. **Click on Print.**

   This step chooses the Print command and displays the Print dialog box. Chart is selected as the item to print. The After screen shows this step.

4. **Click on OK.**

   This step confirms that you want to print; 1-2-3 prints the chart.

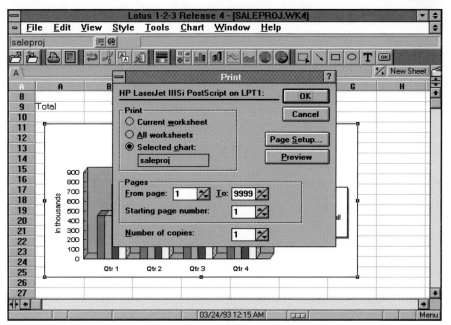

To print the worksheet and the chart, click in the worksheet first. Then choose the File Print command. Then click on OK.

R E V I E W

1. Select the chart.

2. Click on **File** in the menu bar.

3. Click on the **Print** command.

4. Click on **OK**.

To print a chart

Try a shortcut

You can press the Ctrl+P key combination to get the Print dialog box.

Delete a chart

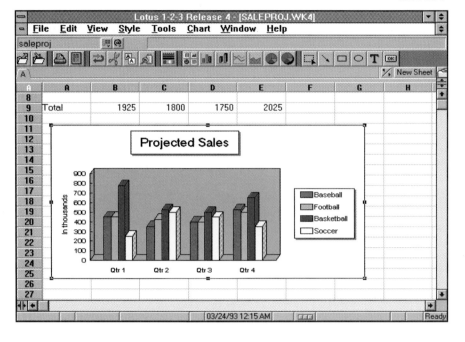

1. **Click on the chart.**

   This step selects the chart. Handles appear along the edges of the chart.

2. **Press Del.**

   Pressing the Del key deletes the chart.

after

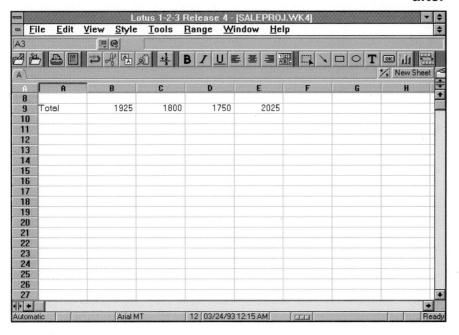

1. Click on the chart to select it.

2. Press **Del**.

To delete a chart

Reference

Quick Reference

Keyboard Guide

Glossary

Where to Get More Help

Easy 1-2-3 for Windows

Quick Reference

If you can't remember how to access a particular feature, use this quick list to find the appropriate menu and command name, or shortcut keystrokes. For more detailed information, take a look at the tasks in the Task/Review part of this book.

Task	Menu options	Shortcut key
Border	Style, Lines & Color	
Center	Style, Alignment, Center	
Close a file	File, Close	
Column Width	Style, Column Width	
Comma format	Style, Number Format, , Comma	
Copy	Edit, Copy	Ctrl+C
Currency Format	Style, Number Format, Currency	
Delete a column	Edit, Delete, Column	Ctrl+-, Column
Delete a row	Edit, Delete, Row	Ctrl+-, Row
Edit		F2
Exit	File, Exit	
Font	Style, Font & Attributes	
Go To	Edit, Go To	F5
Help	Help, Contents	F1
Hide a column	Style, Hide Column	
Insert a column	Edit, Insert, Column	Ctrl++, Column
Insert a row	Edit, Insert, Row	Ctrl++, Row

Task	Menu options	Shortcut key
Left alignment	**Style, Alignment, Left**	
Move	**Edit, Cut, and then Edit, Paste**	**Ctrl+X, Ctrl+V**
New File	**File, New**	
Open a file	**File, Open**	**Ctrl+O**
Patterns	**Style, Lines & Color**	
Preview	**File, Print Preview**	
Print	**File, Print**	**Ctrl+P**
Range Fill	**Range, Fill**	
Range Name	**Range, Name**	
Replace	**Edit, Find & Replace**	
Right align	**Style, Alignment, Right**	
Save	**File, Save**	**Ctrl+S**
Save As	**File, Save As**	
Sort Data	**Range, Sort**	
Undo	**Edit, Undo**	**Ctrl+Z**

Keyboard Guide

Instead of using the mouse with 1-2-3 for Windows, you can use the keyboard. This section covers some basic keyboard operations. For complete instructions on using the keyboard, see *Using 1-2-3 Release 4.0 for Windows,* Special Edition.

To open a menu

Press the Alt key, and then type the underlined letter in the menu name.

To select a menu command

1. Use ↑ or ↓ to move to the command that you want to open.

2. Press Enter.

Or

Type the underlined letter in the menu command name.

To select an option in a dialog box

Press and hold down the Alt key; then type the underlined letter in the check box, text box, list box, option button, or command button. Or you can press the Tab key to scroll through the dialog box options.

To open the 1-2-3 Control menu

Press Alt+space bar.

To select a cell

Use the arrow keys to move to that cell.

To select a range

1. Move the cell pointer to the first cell in the range.

2. Press and hold down the Shift key.

3. Use the arrow keys to highlight the range.

To select OK

Rather than click on the OK button, you can press Enter instead.

Glossary

cell   The intersection of any column and row. Each cell in a worksheet has a unique address. A cell address is formed by combining the worksheet, column, and row locations into one description. For example, A:B8 describes the intersection of column B and row 8 in worksheet A.

cell pointer   An outlined rectangle indicating the active cell. The cell pointer shows where data will be entered or a range will begin.

chart   A visual representation of your data. You can display selected data using one of many chart types—bar chart, pie chart, line chart, and so on.

contents box   The box in the edit line that displays the contents of the cell.

Control menu box   The hyphen or little box that appears in the upper left corner of the title bar of a window. Double-clicking on this box closes the window.

default   The initial settings in effect when you install 1-2-3 for Windows.

dialog box   An on-screen window that displays further command options. Many times a dialog box reminds you of the consequences or results of a command and asks you to confirm that you want to go ahead with the action.

directory   An index to the files stored on disk or a list of files. A directory is similar to folders in a filing cabinet; you can group files together in directories.

DOS   An acronym for *disk operating system*. DOS manages the details of your system—storing and retrieving programs and files.

edit line   The line under the menu bar that contains the selection indicator and the contents box.

file   The various individual reports, memos, databases, and letters that you store on your hard drive (or floppy disk) for future use.

file name   The name that you assign a file when you store it to disk. A file name consists of two parts: the *root* and the *extension*. The root can be up to 8 characters in length. The extension can be 3 characters long and usually indicates the file type. The root and extension are separated by a period. SALES.WK4 is a valid file name. SALES is the root, WK4 is the extension, and the two parts are separated by a period.

floppy disk drive   The door into your computer. The floppy disk drive allows you to put information onto the computer—onto the hard drive—and to take information off the computer—onto a floppy disk.

font   The style, size, and typeface of a set of characters.

formula   An entry that performs a calculation on two or more values in cells.

function   A built-in formula supplied with 1-2-3 for Windows. Functions perform specialized calculations—such as loan payments.

hard disk drive   The device within your system unit that stores the programs and files that you work with.

icon   An on-screen picture that represents a group window, an application, a document, or some other element within windows.

insertion point   The flashing vertical bar that indicates the location of the cursor in a dialog box.

label   A text entry.

menu   An on-screen list of 1-2-3 for Windows options.

menu bar   The line under the title bar that displays menu names.

Microsoft Windows   An operating environment that provides a graphical interface (rather than the DOS character-based interface). A graphical interface helps you learn a computer program more intuitively and use the program more easily. You can use Microsoft Windows to manage your computer system—run programs, copy files, and so on.

mode indicator   A code that appears in the lower right corner of the status bar and indicates the current 1-2-3 program mode.

mouse   An input device that allows you to move the cursor on-screen, select menu commands, and perform other operations.

mouse pointer   The on-screen graphic that moves when you move the mouse.

number format   The way in which values are displayed. You can select to display dollar signs, decimal points, commas, percentages, and so on.

path   The route, through directories, to a program or document file. For instance, the path C:\123W\DATA\REPORT.WK4 includes these elements: the disk drive (C:), the root directory (\), the next directory (123W), the subdirectory (DATA), and the file name (REPORT.WK4).

range   A rectangular area of specified cells. A range can be a cell, a row, a column, or any rectangular area of columns and rows. After you select a range, you can perform many operations on that range—change the font, underline cells, move the range, and so on.

range coordinates   1-2-3 for Windows identifies a range as follows: the first element is the location of the uppermost left cell in the range; the second element is the location of the lowermost right cell. For instance, the range A1..C3 includes the cells A1, A2, A3, B1, B2, B3, C1, C2, and C3.

root directory   The main directory. All other directories are contained in the root directory.

selection indicator   The box on the left side of the edit line that shows the address of the current cell.

SmartIcons   Buttons displayed on the icon palette that provide shortcuts for common tasks—opening a file, changing the format, and so on.

spreadsheet program   An electronic version of an accountant's ledger. A spreadsheet program enables you to enter and manipulate data—calculate, sort, and so on.

status bar   The bottom area of the 1-2-3 for Windows screen. This line displays the current number format, font, and font size, as well as other information.

status indicator   A code that appears in the status bar and tells the current status of the program features. For example, when this indicator displays `Ready`, you know that 1-2-3 is ready for you to issue a command, enter text, and so on.

Undo   A 1-2-3 for Windows feature that enables you to reverse most worksheet changes.

value   A number, formula, date, or time entry.

window   A rectangular area on-screen in which you view a program or a document. A window can contain icons that represent applications, the application itself, or a document you have created in an application.

worksheet   All the data and formatting information you enter on-screen. 1-2-3 for Windows and your operating system keep track of worksheets by storing them on disk in files.

Where to Get More Help

This book does not cover all 1-2-3 for Windows features or all ways of completing each task. This book is geared toward the beginning user—someone who wants just the basics. This person isn't ready for advanced features such as using statistical functions or creating complex databases.

As you become more comfortable with the program, you may need a more complete reference book. *Using 1-2-3 Release 4.0 for Windows*, Special Edition, is an excellent reference that covers all the ins and outs of the program.

You also might find the following titles helpful:

- *Que's Computer User's Dictionary,* 3rd Edition
- *Que's Introduction to Personal Computers,* 3rd Edition
- *Using Windows 3.1,* Special Edition

Index